SHERBORNE

A COTSWOLD VILLAGE

SHERBORNE
A COTSWOLD VILLAGE

Sybil Longhurst • *Walter Tufnell* • *Alice Tufnell*

ALAN SUTTON

First published in the United Kingdom in 1992
Alan Sutton Publishing Ltd · Phoenix Mill · Far Thrupp · Stroud · Gloucestershire

First published in the United States of America in 1992
Alan Sutton Publishing Inc · Wolfeboro Falls · NH 03896–0848

British Library Cataloguing in Publication Data

Longhurst, Sybil
Sherborne: A Cotswold Village
I. Title
942.417

ISBN 0 7509 0081 4

Library of Congress Cataloging in Publication Data applied for

Cover photograph: Sherborne, Bottom End, *c.* 1925.

Typeset in Times 10/12
Typesetting and origination by
Alan Sutton Publishing Limited.
Printed in Great Britain by
The Bath Press, Avon.

We would like to dedicate this book
to the memory of our co-author
Walter Scott Tufnell
who unfortunately passed away before
the book reached publication.

Contents

Illustrations

Sherborne, Bottom End, before 1910.

View of the Bottom End of Sherborne.

CHAPTER ONE

The Village – Setting the Scene

The village of Sherborne, unlike many of its neighbours, appears today as a quiet backwater, yet this has not always been the case, for this attractive Cotswold village was once a bustling and thriving centre of the medieval wool trade. The lords of the manor, the Duttons, were an influential family who had connections with both Elizabeth I and Oliver Cromwell, and for many years owned extensive estates throughout Gloucestershire.

The first recording of 'Scireburne' (meaning a clear stream or brook) is in the Domesday Book of 1086. It describes the village as being divided into an 'Eastende' and 'Westende', separated by the manor belonging to the Abbey of Winchcombe. Over the years the pronunciation of the village name seems to have altered little, though the attempts to spell it vary from Schirborne in 1191, Shirbourn in 1349 and Schyreburn in 1405 to Schireborne in 1776.

The general layout of the village has not altered in nine hundred years; the eastern half of the village is now known to the locals as 'Bottom End' and the western half as 'Top End'. The Domesday Book also refers to the village as having had four mills.

The present village comprises seventeenth- and eighteenth-century houses, plus rows of nineteenth-century cottages built in the east end as part of a 'model village' plan. In 1954 twelve council houses were added at the Top End, and three later additions were Brookfield House at Waterloo, The Orchard by The Kennels and Prescott in the old timber yard.

EARLY HISTORY

Mesolithic people of Nordic stock, with fair hair and fair complexions, are thought to have been the first settlers in the Cotswolds. Then followed neolithic immigrants from the Mediterranean region who buried their dead in long barrows. One of these, near Lodge Park in the south-west of Sherborne parish, was opened just after the Second World War and found to be empty – presumably the target of some previous disturbance.

The Dobunni, who were later occupants of the area, were known to grow corn and keep sheep, cattle and pigs. An uneasy peace was negotiated when the Romans

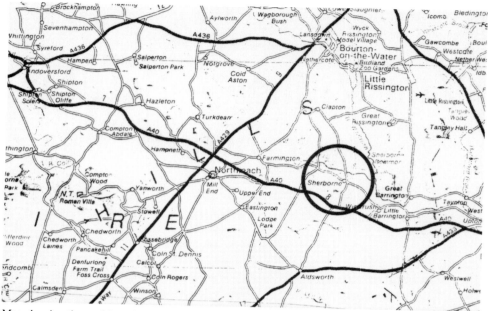

Map showing the position of Sherborne.

arrived in the region and nearby Corinium (Cirencester), the largest town after London, became the new capital of Britannia Prima.

The traces still survive today of Roman villas in the nearby villages of Great Barrington and Farmington, which were served by the Fosse Way, one of the best remaining examples of Roman roads, and passing five miles to the west of Sherborne.

The West Saxons and Angles followed the Roman infiltration of the Dobunni territory and, by the end of the seventh century, monasteries had appeared in the area in Gloucester, Bath, Tetbury, Withington and Malmesbury. The Abbey of Winchcombe, which was to become the original owner of the manor and village of Sherborne, was founded in 798 by King Kenwulf of Mercia.

Sherborne was, by all accounts, a profitable holding and the leasing of it in 1533 for a rent of 'one peppercorn' per annum seems to have been an attempt to forestall the depredation caused by Henry VIII's dissolution of the monasteries. The lease, which was for ninety-nine years, was held by Sir John Alleyn, Lord Mayor of London. Christopher, his son, also held the manor.

POPULATION

The size of Sherborne village has varied considerably over the centuries. In the Domesday Book the population is recorded as fifty-nine landholders plus families. By 1355 there were fifty-four landholders in the East End and thirty-seven in the

West End, giving a total population of approximately three hundred. Rents at this time varied between 6d. and 2s. per annum.

In 1661 the village consisted of five freeholders and thirty-six tenants. The family of John Humphries, who was living in the village at this time, had been free tenants since the thirteenth century. John may even have been a descendant of the Humphrey of Sherborne who held land in fee in 1166.

Numbering 767, the population of Sherborne seems to have reached its peak in 1831, at the time of the rebuilding of Sherborne House and village. Since that time numbers have gradually dropped from 584 in 1861 and 430 in 1951 to 286 in 1976.

AMENITIES

In 1660 There was a smithy, a weaver, a tiler, a ploughmaker, a carpenter and a wheelwright.

In 1755 There were two alehouses.

In 1863 *Kelly's Directory* records the following workmen in the village:

Robert Collet	– blacksmith
John Webber Hewer	– draper, grocer and sub-postmaster
Thomas Kench	– shopkeeper
William Margetts	– carpenter
Edmund Rous	– shoemaker
Elisha Smith	– baker at Sherborne Mill
John Tate	– tailor
Thomas Whinam	– builder
John Hitchman	– alehouse
John Leech	– alehouse

The suretor of the two alehouses was John Hartwell of Bourton-on-the-Water. The licence was dated 13 September 1755 and cost £10 0s. 0d.

The present-day amenities include:

Penny Collins	– shopkeeper and sub-postmistress
Ian Long	– carpenter
Stuart Ferris	– cabinet maker
Derek Elliot	– cabinet maker
Les and Dave Hayward	– builders
John Hill	– landscape gardener
	– Sherborne Garden Centre
E.P. Yiangou	– architect

CHAPTER TWO

Topography, Flora and Fauna

The village of Sherborne lies six miles west of Burford, three miles east of Northleach and four miles south of Bourton-on-the-Water, the nearest sizeable towns being Cirencester, fourteen miles to the south and Cheltenham, seventeen miles west.

The majority of the village is built on the south side of Sherborne Brook. This tributary of the Windrush rises in Cold Aston, runs underground until it rises again near Farmington, and then joins the Windrush at the east end of the parish.

Nestling in a valley, the village has ground rising to 700 feet on the north side and to 600 feet on the south.

The rock around Sherborne, from which many of the cottages in the village are constructed, is inferior oolitic limestone, rich in fossils. This stone bestows its beauty on the village buildings.

Many flowers which were commonly found in the 1920s and 1930s are now quite rare. Included among those are: green hellebore, common hellebore, fly orchid, bee orchid, early purple orchids, sanfoin, meadow saffron, lily of the valley, primrose, milkwort, rock rose, wild thyme, sorrel and moon daisy.

Badgers, foxes, field mice, voles and moles are still plentiful among the mammals. Even wild fallow deer are often seen in the woods and fields, but the otter, once common on the river banks, is very rarely seen today.

Bird varieties too have suffered, some almost to extinction. These include little owls, barn owls, sparrowhawks and buzzards, but attempts are being made to increase these populations. A decrease in the activities of gamekeepers has led to a rise in the numbers of kestrels, magpies, crows and jays. There are large numbers of pheasant, blackbirds, thrushes, chaffinches, goldfinches and tits of all varieties to be seen.

Pipistrelle bats are often seen in the early evening twilight and there is a colony of lesser horseshoe bats on the Sherborne estate, but other bat species are seldom seen.

During the summer months the fields are ablaze with colour as butterflies flutter away their short winged life. Commas, adonis blues and various other blues are common. Large white, small white, marbled white, meadow brown, orange tip, painted ladies, peacocks, red admiral, ringlet, small tortoiseshell and speckled wood are other varieties that adorn the flowers. In 1985 a stir was caused when a colony of the rare Duke of Burgundy was discovered, a national newspaper ran the following report:

Numbers 47 and 48 Sherborne, about 1908.

The National Trust nature experts are all of a flutter after finding a colony of rare brown and cream butterflies. This discovery of the Duke of Burgundy Butterfly has forced a big tree-clearing operation on the Sherborne Estate – because the insects do not like being under cover. The lava feed on Cowslips in fairly tall grass which needs open, unshaded space to grow. 'There are not many locations outside the Cotswolds, so we are glad we can do something to conserve the colony,' said Mr. Alexander the National Trust Estate Advisory Officer.

The village is well wooded with many varieties of trees: larch, scots pine, yew, great willow, crack willow, white willow, aspen, walnut, silver birch, alder, hornbeam, hazel, beech, sweet chestnut, horse chestnut, sycamore, field maple, holly, common lime, ash, species of oak, cedar, and wych elm (a great number of elm trees thrived until Dutch elm disease struck and virtually wiped out the species).

ROADS

The roads through the village have changed position over the years, indeed it is likely that the original road from Oxford to Gloucester passed directly through Sherborne at one time.

When the Turnpike Act was passed in 1751, Lord Sherborne, who had a vested

Mr J. Howard, carter for Mr R. Houlton, Mill Hill Farm during the early 1900s. Waterloo Bridge is in the background.

interest in the spa at Cheltenham, was a strong advocate for building the new 'Ridgeway' (now the A40), which was completed in 1753.

In 1822 a new road was built from Clapton-on-the-Hill to the east end of the village, and then on up to the Ridgeway. The portion from the east end to the A40 is still known locally as 'New Road'. Thus, the road known variously as Home Farm Lane, Tyte Lane (there was possibly a tithe barn nearby) and Station Road, running from the post office past Home Farm to the Ridgeway, became virtually redundant. The name Station Road derived from the hope of a railway line being built parallel to the Ridgeway, however objections from neighbouring landowners thwarted this possibility.

In 1856 the road from Sherborne to Farmington was diverted to its present location. Northleach Lane, the road leading from the A40 through the west end of the village to Bourton-on-the-Water crossroads (also known as Coal House Corner), is believed to have been built in the late eighteenth century.

BRIDGES

There are four stone bridges in the Sherborne parish: Haycroft Bridge, Waterloo Bridge, the Cascade Bridge and Walestone or Wadlestone Bridge.

Haycroft Bridge is the tallest and perhaps the most elegant, and links Haycroft House to the Farmington Road.

There is evidence that before Waterloo Bridge was built in the eighteenth century, a ford, which bears a bench mark, existed to the east of the bridge site. The bridge was built to convey traffic across Sherborne Brook on the Ridgeway to the Bourton Road.

The Cascade Bridge was built on top of a weir, the first weir on the Sherborne Brook. To the eastern side of the bridge is a shallow cobbled ford which is still used to this day.

Walestone or Wadlestone is the longest of the four bridges and was built to complete the road from Clapton to the Ridgeway through the east end of Sherborne. It has railings on one side and a stone wall on the other, and underneath has varying sized arches. There is a walled-up stone stile and stone pillars, the eastern one of which is marked with the inscription: 'T.L. 1787', together with a scratch mark. This is presumably the spot where Sherborne Brook was crossed by another ford.

CHAPTER THREE

Trade and Agriculture

COTSWOLD STONE

The vast majority of houses in Sherborne were built from local stone and, in the Middle Ages, Cotswold-stone slates were in regular use.

There are several traces of free-stone quarries throughout the parish. In early days, stone was taken from the south of the park where 'caves' can still be seen. Most of the dry stone for building and walling was, in later times, taken from Cat's (St Catherine's) Abbey quarry at the south-east end of the parish.

Sherborne stone was used for several notable projects and was transported considerable distances for this purpose. William of Wykeham, overseer of Windsor Castle in the reign of Edward III, had as his clerk of works Richard Taynton, who used stone from Sherborne for the royal lodges. Droves of oxen conveyed stone from Sherborne to London when St Paul's Cathedral was being built, a journey which took six weeks. In the late seventeenth century an old sloping weir was made, in the River Windrush at Little Barrington, to assist barges carrying stone from Sherborne quarries.

Gravel was another product of the village. When the Broadwater and Cascade were made in Sherborne Brook, the thousands of tons of gravel that were removed were taken to Bristol to assist in making Avonmouth Docks – this fact was recorded in *The King's England*, Gloucestershire.

BRICK AND TILE WORKS

It is recorded that, in the nineteenth century, there was a brick and tile works in Sherborne. This industry finally closed in 1902.

Although a few houses in the village still retain the red 'Sherborne' roofing tiles, sadly the numbers have decreased over the years.

THE WOOL TRADE

After the Norman Conquest, as peace and prosperity came to the land, the English began to export wool to Flanders, the Netherlands and Italy.

Cotswold sheep, in particular, were noted for their large size, long necks and pure white fleeces. One of Sherborne's four mills, described in the Domesday Book as a 'fulling mill', would have played an important role in the cleaning and

No. 88 Sherborne, showing the Norman
doorway, reputed to have been taken from
the old Church or Chapel which once stood
in what is now the garden of Stones Farm.

whitening of these fleeces. The actual location of the fulling mill is now uncertain, but it was used extensively in the early fourteenth century when the Abbot of Winchcombe had a cut made to improve the flow of water. A large seam of fuller's earth, located in the land to the south of the river provided Sherborne with this important material for the process.

By the fourteenth and fifteenth centuries the wool trade had reached a peak. Wool from the upland manors of Snowshill, Charlton Abbots, Roel and Hawling was taken to Sherborne where the peasants would wash the fleeces and sew them into packs of two hundred or more. The only reward the peasants received for their labours was a food allowance and, on completion of the work, a shearing feast was provided.

In 1380 Cotswold wool sold at 9s. 4d. per tod (47p for approximately 28 lbs) increasing to 13s. 4d. (67p) per tod by 1481. This remarkably good price, almost three times that of wool from other locations in England, reflected the high quality of the product. Sadly, subsequent years saw a fall in the prices until eventually they reached a par with those in the rest of the country.

For many years during the fifteenth century, the Abbot of Winchcombe moved his entire household to Sherborne for the month of May. The reason for this thirteen-mile journey on horseback can be seen when it is realized that in 1485 alone, nearly three thousand sheep were sheared at Sherborne. The whole process took four days and filled fourteen sacks. The following 1485 accounts still exist on parchment roll:

And in victuals bought at the time of shearing and dipping the sheep   24s. 4d.
Paid several men for bringing the sheep to the dipping and shearing   2s. 4d.
Paid one woman working in the kitchen   2s. 4d.
Paid for shepherds   2s.
Paid William Smith for sorting fourteen sacks of wool   16s. 4d.
Paid for the packing of the said wool with victuals and wages provided 14s. 2d.
Paid for dipping and shearing 2,900 sheep   67s. 3d.

In 1436 Bernard of Lombardy, a wool merchant from Italy, visited Sherborne on a regular basis and exported his wool purchases to the Continent via Calais. It is assumed, however, that most of the Sherborne wool was traded through William Midwinter, who was the principle dealer for the Northleach area. Richard Celey, another merchant of the staple, had a business in London and bought wool from the Northleach region. This wool was taken by pack-horse across country via Newbury to Southampton docks and loaded on to galleys, freshly bereft of their cargoes of silks and spices, for onward transmission to Calais. Once the wool was offloaded at Calais, Richard Celey's son became responsible for its disposal.

The high regard in which Cotswold wool was held throughout this period was illustrated when, during the reign of Edward IV, the king of Portugal made a special request for leave to export sixty sacks to weave into gold cloth for court ceremonies – perhaps some Sherborne fleeces were among those sent?

MILLS

In the twelfth century a mill was granted, by the abbot, to John Hastings of Farmington, on the condition that it was not to be turned into a fulling mill. It was to be sited near his land, in Sherborne. A house and 1 acre of land was granted with it. This mill was probably the one known as Stagges Mill (and possibly later as Ducklestone Mill) which was held by the lord of Farmington at a rent of 13s. 4d. in 1355. William Fifield held it by free tenure and, upon his death in 1405, his son paid a relief and a heriot of an ox for it.

In the mid-fourteenth century there also appears to have been three corn mills in the area. One was held freely with two yardlands (a yard of land was about 30 acres) and a meadow, the other two being held by customary tenants at a rent of 13s. 4d. The more valuable fulling mill attracted an annual rent of 16s. In 1391 a mill was taken off the lord's lands, because the miller had let it deteriorate.

In 1803 William Cross occupied a mill, possibly Ducklestone, hence the barn which stood opposite acquired the name of Cross's Barn (which was converted into a house in 1988 by Lady Cromwell, who owns the Oranges Farm).

By the end of the nineteenth century the sole remaining mill became known finally as Ducklestone Mill. The early part of the twentieth century saw the mill used as a bakery, owned and occupied by a Mr Howard. The Broad family, who succeeded Mr Howard, then ran a smallholding at the mill. When they left it was used purely as a dwelling and remains so to this day.

Sheep shearing on Home Farm, in the early 1900s.

FARMING

Sherborne has always been an agricultural area. The earliest records are taken from the Domesday Book of 1086, when the Abbey of Winchcombe owned the holding (as the village was then called). The holding was about 30 hides (a hide being approximately 120 acres) in size. Ten of the hides were free, belonging to the demesne (court) for supplying the Abbey House. The court had 5 ploughs (5 teams of oxen), there were 40 villeins (villagers) and 7 borderii (cottagers or smallholders) who had 22 ploughs, 12 servii (slaves), 4 mills at 40s. and a meadow of 30 acres. In all the value of the holding was approximately £14.

There is a large old house, known as Monks Farm House, at the west end of the village, complete with cellars, attics and an old serving hatch. During restoration work carried out a few years ago, a painting of a man and a dog was revealed on one of the walls. Thought to be the work of artists in the sixteenth century, the painting is in almost perfect condition.

In 1222 the abbot was paid 40s. a year for tithing at Sherborne.

In 1327, according to the Gloucestershire subsidy roll, thirty-eight tenants paid a total of 56s. 7d. (£2.83) in taxes. The levy varied from 6d. to 10s. The tenants only paid tax if their assessed movable wealth exceeded 15s. Historians calculate that, by using a multiple of four and a half, the population at this time would have been around the 180 mark.

In 1355, 1 tenant farmed 200 acres, 23 tenants had 100 acres each and 33 tenants had 40 acres each, and there were also a few other smallholders.

According to the *Victoria County History of Gloucestershire*, in 1445 there was a ploughmaker and a tiler living in the village.

Between 1450 and 1500, there were 400 acres planted with crops of wheat, peas, beans, oats and dredge corn for beer. Most of these crops went to the abbey.

In 1464 the manor estate was 'farmed out' to Richard Arderne, who ran it on a two-field system: Cowham and its surroundings – referred to as 'Northfield' (still identified by two cottages and barns to the north-east of the village); and Manor Farm, with buildings behind the present church, known as 'Southfield'. The farmer, who was responsible for the abbey's sheep when they were in Sherborne, paid a cash rent and acted as rent collector for the other tenants. Farming was done on the three-year rotation method: year one, oats, barley and fallow; year two, grazing; and year three, fallow, oats and barley.

The numbers of sheep increased to a shearing peak of 2,900 in 1485 (in fact there was only sufficient water in Sherborne Brook to wash 3,000 sheep).

SHERBORNE COMPOTUS ROLL

The account of Brother John Lenche, collector of the rents and farm of the manor of Sherborne, in Gloucestershire. Balance sheet at 29 September 1484.

PAYMENTS

1. Resolute Rents: To the Sacrist [keeper of the goods and ornaments] of the Parish Church of St John the Baptist at Cirencester, in the payment of an Annual rent for providing a Free School there   £10 0s. 0d.

2. Purchase of Grain and Stock: To Alice Stratford for tithe grain of the Rectory there from her purchased, and there remaining for the use of The Lord Abbot   £10. 0s. 0d.
   To Thomas Lake for five oxen   £3 8s. 4d.
   To Alice Stratford for two oxen   £1 8s. 0d.
   To Nicholas Gylys for one ox   12s. 8d.
   To John Hanks for two oxen   £1 9s. 0d.

   £16 18s. 0d. £16 18s. 0d.

3. Purchase of necessaries: To Alice Stratford for one pair of wheels, with their appendages   15s. 4d.
   For one canvas (sheet) for winnowing grain   3s. 4d.
   For four pairs of Traces   1s. 8d.
   For two horse collars   1s. 3d.
   For 12 yards of cloth for making sacks   2s. 6d.

   £1 4s. 1d.

   For a lamp   10d.
   " 2 'Bonches Alij'   1s. 0d.
   " 2 Sieves   8d.
   " 2 Small sieves   8d.
   " 2 Iron 'towes' [? tools]   1s. 8d.
   " 2 Knives   1s. 9d.
   " 2 Ploughshares   1s. 8d.
   " 4 'Pedalipz fferren' [iron clogs]   1s. 0d.
   " Iron chain for the horse plough   4d.
   " 2 Iron bills and laxe   1s. 2d.
   " 2 Dungpicks   8d.
   " 1 Brandart   1s. 6d.
   " 18 yards of Cicilian Cloth called hair   6s. 0d.
   " Expenses at Stow Fair   4d.

   £2 3s. 4d. £26 18s. 0d.

   B/F   £26 18s. 0d.

For 4 Horseshoes		6d.
" Nails for the horses		3d.
" A. Sedelipp [for sowing]		4d.
" White leather		10d.
" Pipis [staves for the horses]		3d.
" Cord		2d.
" Nails and 200 laths		10d.
" Ironwork	2s.	7d.
" A measure	1s.	0d.
" Halters		6d.
" 4 yokes and yoking poles	1s.	4d.
" 2 ploughs	3s.	0d.
" Timber for the ploughs	4s.	0d.
" Smith's wages for divers necessaries as appears by tally	2s.	11d.
" Threshing the grain	1s.	8d.
" Women working at the plough	3s.	0d.
" 1 'Butler'		4d.
" A load of 'Sclatt' [slates]	1s.	0d.
" Travelling expenses	1s.	0d.

£3 8s. 10d.   £30 6s. 10d.

                B/F   £30 6s. 10d.

4. Washing and shearing of sheep:

For victuals bought during the washing and shearing	£1 9s.	4d.
To men for carrying the sheep at the washing and shearing	2s.	4d.
To a woman collecting the fleeces for four days		6d.
To a woman working in the kitchen		4d.
To four shepherds for coming and assisting at shearing time	2s.	0d.
To Richard Smith for 'le Tryndynge' fourteen sacks of wool	16s.	4d.
For packing said wool, with victuals and wages given	14s.	2d.
For washing and shearing 2,900 sheep as appears by parcel of said account	£3 7s.	3d.

£6 12s. 3d. £36 19s. 1d.

                B/F   £36 19s. 1d.

5. Expenses of servants:
   For expenses of William Merriett, Bailiff, for the term of St Michael as follows:

For corn	4s. 0d.	
" bread	1s. 1d.	
" malt	8s. 9d.	
" carcases of oxen	2s. 9d.	
" one sheep	1s. 8d.	
" one cheese	1s. 6d.	
" hens eggs	9d.	
" lard	1d.	
" candles	5d.	
" shoeing of horses	1s. 1d.	
" 4 bushels of corn	2s. 0d.	
" 6 bushels of malt	2s. 6d.	
" carcases of oxen and sheep	6s. 4d.	
" candles	7d.	

£1 13s. 7d.*   £38 12s. 8d.

B/F   £38 12s. 8d.

6. Mowing of the Meadow: £1 6s. 8d.
   To four men for mowing the Lord's meadow, there
   called Medelham paid them as for price of
   4 bushels of malt   1s. 8d.
   To men and women haymakers for tedding the hay   11s. 10d.
   For carcases of sheep and oxen bought at the same
   time   1s. 4d.
   For cheese   1s. 1d.
   For milk   4d.

£2 2s. 11d.

7. Wages of Servants (on dorse of roll):
   Wages of William Herriette, Bailiff   11s. 4d.
   For another man for same time   6s. 8d.
   For another servant   6s. 0d.
   For the ploughman for two weeks   2s. 0d.
   For a woman driving the plough for eight days   8d.
   For a man working there for two days   4d.

£1 7s. 0d. £42 2s. 7d.

B/F   £42 2s. 7d.

* Brother Lenche's sum is in error here, the pence should be 6d.

Sherborne Post Office and No. 38 in the late 1920s. From left, Albert Townsend, Mr & Mrs H. Taylor, Mrs Hayward, Harry Taylor (standing on wall), Winnie George, Lionel Cyphus (seated on wall), Mrs Ethel Jones and Mrs Elsie Taylor.

8. Livery of Moneys:
   Handed to Thomas Forthey, Bailiff there, charged
   on this account by the hands of Thomas Lake   £2 11s. 8d.
   To the same as for the price of 4 quarters of seed
   barley   9s. 0d.

                                               £3 0s. 8d. £45 3s. 3d.

                             B/F   £45 3s. 3d.

9. Addenda:
   Paid Richard Hobbs for collecting divers crops there
   this year   5s. 0d.
   For 2 quarters of seed corn   10s. 6d.
   For 4 bushels of Pulse for keep of the pigs   1s. 0d.

                                               16s. 6d. £45 19s. 9d.
                 Total Expenditure   £45 19s. 9d.

RECEIPTS

1. Farm of the Manor:
   From the Farm of the Manor of Sherborne, with its
   lands, meadows, fields and pastures as demised to
   Richard Stratford at farm for the term of 20 years,
   this year being the tenth, excepting certain meadows
   and pastures reserved to The Lord Abbot's use
   during the afforsaid, at yearly rent   £13 6s. 8d.
   Of issues of the Dovecot nothing is charged, as it
   remains in the Abbot's hands, whereof the House
   Steward will answer in his Account   £0 0s. 0d.
   Nor of a close at 10s. farm called Hickcombehey,
   nothing accounted for here because included in the
   farm rent   £0 0s. 0d.
   Nor of 20s. for Tithes of the Manor, nothing
   accounted for here because it was assigned to said
   Richard Stratford for corn and malt and providing
   provender for the horses during the annual washing
   and shearing of the Lord's sheep there   £0 0s. 0d. £13 6s. 8d.

                                                          £13 6s. 8d.

2. Sales of the Meadows:
   From the farm of a meadow called Cowham, with all
   the parcels of hay and the second crop of the said
   meadow for this year, as demised to the said Richard
   Stratford at farm   £8 0s. 0d.   £8 0s. 0d.

   _____

                                                                             £21 6s. 8d.

3. Issues of the Manor:
   From the farm of the Dovecot and the crop of the
   Lord's Park there yearly   10s. 0d.   10s. 0d.

   _____

                                                                             £21 16s. 8d.

4. Farm of the Rectory:
   From the farm of the Rectory there, as demised to
   the said Richard Stratford for the term of twenty
   years, yearly   £10 0s. 0d.   £10 0s. 0d.

   _____

                                                                             £31 16s. 8d.
                                                                             £14 3s. 1d.
                         Defecit ....

   _____

                                                                             £45 19s. 9d.

In 1608, according to the record of 'Men and Armour' for Gloucestershire, there
were eighty-three male inhabitants of Sherborne who were able to practise military
skills in the following roles: calyvers, pikemen, musketeers and pioneers. These
men were mainly husbandmen (farmers who were tillers of the land), yeomen
(smallholders), milners (?millers), sheppeards (shepherds), and the remainder
were labourers and servants. Twenty-three of these men were employed by William
Dutton Esq. in one form or another.

By 1622, 1,017 acres of pasture and meadow had been enclosed.

In 1658 an agreement had been reached, between the inhabitants of the Top and
Bottom Ends of the village, about which area of the brook was their responsibility
for keeping free from weeds.

A carpenter and wheelwright were established in the village by 1660.

In 1661 it was determined that, at thirty sheep per yardland holding, the common
lands were overstocked and reductions had to be made to a maximum of twenty.
Tenants were permitted one horse per yardland, but no mares. In Gloucestershire a
yardland comprised approximately 30 acres.

Garne is a very well-known name connected with sheep in this area. The first
mention of it was in 1648 when a Thomas Garne bought two 'messuages' (dwelling
houses with outbuildings and land) and four yardlands from John ('Crump')
Dutton.

According to *A Six Weeks Tour Through The Southern Counties Of England And
Wales* (published by W. Nicoll, 51 St Paul's Churchyard, London, 1768), a

writer/traveller from the eastern counties (believed to be one, Arthur Young) journeyed through the locality in 1768 and complained about the state of the road between Witney and Northleach. He wrote:

> The country is open, dull and disagreeable, the crops generally are poor and full of weeds, the fallows the same, all bad husbandry. They use foot ploughs with one wheel and four horses in length, and plough an acre a day. They reckon three quarters of wheat, barley or beans a good crop [a quarter of grain was 8 bushels, the standard measure used for corn and meal until the end of the nineteenth century]. The farms are abundantly large and the farmhouses are all in the towns [villages]. Enclosing is scarce, Mr Dutton has started some at Sherborne, but the scheme goes on very slowly. All this bleak, unpleasant country would be fit for any kind of trees which would yield considerable profit, where firing is scarce. Coal can be bought from Gloucester at twenty five shillings [£1.25] a ton.
> Prices paid for labour in Winter and Spring 8 pence to 10 pence per day. Summer one shilling, Harvest 1s. 8d., Mowing Barley 6d. per acre. Butter is dear at 7½d. per pound.

Perhaps Mr Dutton read this traveller's report and was stirred into action by the critical words therein, because by 1777 many of the large, open fields were enclosed. This gave rise to approximately one hundred fields which were given names to identify them as to their ownership and to assist in keeping records of cropping. The names of Cowham and Picardy are still in evidence. Picardy, to the north of the river, was first mentioned in the Domesday Book: it is recorded, in 1445, that it was enclosed by a ditch. A wood and ditch are still in existence in the parish. The field now named Cowham is most likely to be that referred to as Culham in 1221. Haughcroft, adjacent to the Clapton road, by the river, was referred to as Heurcroft in 1186 and Heycroft in 1540.

A requirement of the Enclosure Act was that persons allocated land were responsible for the cost of fencing off the fields either by ditch, hedge, fence or wall. Mr Dutton was responsible for the charge of enclosing Sherborne land which cost him a total of £86 14s.

The Act also decreed that roads should be made from the centre of the village to the parish boundaries, and thus the village shop was born. The roads enabled the 'bagmen' to travel through the villages and display their wares, and shopkeepers to travel to the markets to buy stock in suitable quantities.

By the early 1800s Sherborne was divided into six farms. Three were around the outskirts – Broadmoor, Haycroft and Woeful Lake – and three within the village – Home Farm, Stones and Sherborne Farm – all complete with cottages and barns. An old ledger reveals that, in 1836, the estate still extended as far as Northleach, Farmington and Eastington. Perhaps surprisingly, three females were tenants of farms in Sherborne: Mrs Elizabeth Cross at the Mill, Mrs Sarah Stephens at Haycroft (the 'Mrs' was a courtesy title) and Widow Gillett at Woeful Lake.

It was interesting to note from this ledger that sainfoin and turnips registered the highest acreage, followed by barley.

In 1820 Thomas Garne (born in 1791) married Mary Gillett, daughter of the farmer at Woeful Lake. Five years later Thomas took over tenancy of Broadmoor Farm. To quote from *Cotswold Yeomen and Sheep*, a book by Richard Garne, the great, great grandson of Thomas, 'Thomas was an outstanding cattle breeder. He kept Longhorn cattle which were used for beef, milk and as draught oxen then changed to Shorthorns which had recently been introduced to the district. He showed at local shows and exported bulls to Canada and Australia.'

When Thomas Garne died in 1873 the sale of his Shorthorn cattle averaged 81 guineas each. Thomas was buried in Sherborne churchyard.

Thomas's eldest son, William Gillett Garne, assumed control of Broadmoor, a position for which he had been groomed. In 1852 William had married Mary Houlton, daughter of the head gamekeeper on the Sherborne estate.

In 1875 grain was being imported from America, and large quantities of wool, imported from the Colonies, resulted in a fall in farm prices. Barley was showing a better profit than wool, root crops were being introduced to supplement feed for stock, thus cutting down the land available for pasture, so inevitably the number of sheep began to decline. Due to the very wet summers in the 1880s resulting in poor harvests, plus an outbreak of liver fluke in sheep, many farmers on the Cotswolds became bankrupt. One who suffered this fate was William G. Garne of Broadmoor, and the result was a farm sale of all his live and deadstock on 22 and 23 March 1882.

Mr Richard Garne quotes, 'The sale consisted of 400 Cotswold and Oxford Down sheep, 34 head of Shorthorn cattle, 18 horses plus donkeys, pigs, poultry and bees. A steam engine, thrashing machine, corn mill, elevator and cattle float, sundry agricultural implements, dairy utensils and effects sold by Acock, Hanks and Garne.'

As William and Mary had no family of their own, William's cousin Richard Garne took over the tenancy of Broadmoor. He bred good Cotswold sheep which won first prize at the Smithfield Show of 1888. He also bred Shorthorn cattle which averaged 45 guineas a piece at sale. Upon Richard's death in 1897, the Garne occupancy of Broadmoor ended.

Between 1897 and 1900 a narrow strip of trees was planted in each field between Vincents Lodge and Radbournes Corner, expanding the belt alongside the Ridgeway (A40). In 1900 Century Wood was planted on Sherborne Farm, a small stone, inside the wood entrance, commemorates the event.

In days of old it had been quite acceptable for women and boys to work full-time on the land, as they were a source of cheap labour. However, during the nineteenth century boys started to attend school, and this attendance was increased towards the latter end of the century in preference to working the land for a pittance.

At the start of the twentieth century wages were still very low, indeed, in 1911 there were 18 employees (16 men and 2 boys) working on Home Farm for a total weekly wage of £12 17s. 6d. The highest-paid employee was Leonard Cyphus (the herdsman) who collected £1 per week, while the other men received between 12s. and 18s. and the boys' wages were 6s. 6d. and 8s. respectively. Mr Broad, shepherd at Home Farm in 1911, received 14s. per week, plus his house.

A copy of a 'Contract of Hiring', dated 31 March 1914 (opposite), gives us a further

CONTRACT OF HIRING.

Name of Master *Frederic Arkell*

Residence *Northleach Glos*

Name of Servant *Alfred Larner*

Residence *Farmington Northleach*

Hired to *Michaelmas 1914.* from *Ladyday 1914*

WAGES *15/- per week? Cottage Potato Grd £1 for Haymaking £1 for Harvest*

To serve as a *Shepherd* and fill up his time at anything he may be required to do, and continue working in Haymaking and Harvest as long as he may be required.

If Absent from Illness or other cause Wages to be deducted.

This agreement is made especially subject to the said *Alfred Larner* receiving from his last Employer a character satisfactory to the said *F. Arkell*

(Signed) *F. Arkell* Master.

alfred Larner Servant.

Dated *March 31st* Earnest Money *1/-*

A contract of hiring for Alfred Larner made in 1914.

insight into wages and conditions of employment. The contract was drawn up between Mr Frederick Arkell, a farmer at Farmington, and his shepherd, Alfred Larner. The period of hiring included Michaelmas (29 September) to Ladyday (25 March) and the wages negotiated were 15s. per week, plus cottage and ground to plant potatoes. An extra payment of £1 was to be paid for haymaking and also for harvest. When Mr Larner was not busy as shepherd, he was to be usefully employed at other labours. During haymaking and harvest he was to continue working as long as may be required. If absent through illness or other causes, his wages would be deducted.

During the same period, oxen were still used as draught animals, but they were gradually being phased out and replaced by horses. The man who handled the horses was known as a carter. In the mild weather, the carter's day started between 5 a.m. and 6 a.m., when the horses that had been turned out into the field the previous evening had to be brought into the stables to be fed and watered. The carter, if he lived nearby, then returned home to his breakfast and to collect his lunch while the horses were feeding. On returning to the stable, the carter's next task was to harness the horses and ensure that his trousers were 'hitched up' and tied just below the knee to prevent them dragging in the mud. During threshing days all the farm workers ensured their trousers were tied in this way to stop rats or mice venturing up their legs. (An agricultural worker would never be without his pocket/shut knife and pieces of string.) In the summer months ear caps, made from beautifully embroidered and tassled, unbleached calico, were placed over the

Mr Arch Jones ploughing on Home Farm; note the embroidered ear caps on the horses.

Mr Valence, a student on Mr W. Tremaine's Farm in the early 1900s. A horse called Bob is between the shafts.

horses' ears to prevent the flies worrying them. The carter's lunch bag and horses' nosebags were hung on the harness and all would be ready to start work by 7 a.m. As both men and beasts covered many miles during the course of a day, breaks for meals were most welcome. While the horses snuffled into their nosebags, the men would consume hunks of bread and cheese, or a piece of fat home-cured bacon with an onion, cut with a pocket knife into edible portions. His usual drink was a bottle of cold, sweetened, black tea (the thermos flask being a thing of the future).

At haymaking and harvest time the menfolk were often joined by their wives and children for tea, and these meal times were punctuated by local gossip and friendly banter. These were regarded as fun times and were looked forward to as a chance to stop and relax for a while, indeed even slices of bread and jam tasted better eaten out in the fields, rather than sitting round the kitchen table.

Wives and children would spend the summer evenings gleaning any loose ears of corn into sacks, which were then taken to the nearest miller for grinding, or scattered among the poultry. The barley meal was used to fatten the pig in the sty, while the wheat flour was used for baking.

When the corn was cut by old-fashioned binders, the lads who would meet on the hill at the Bottom End of the village would ask, 'D'ust know if ther be any binding goin' on?'. A reply could be, 'Ah, Tremaines be at it in the Devil's Dancin' Ground', alternatively, 'Strattons be at it in the Hitchin'', or 'Blakes 'ull soon finish in Take In'. After a brief discussion, armed with sticks, they would be off, with two or maybe even three on one bicycle, one on the saddle, one on the crossbar and one on the carrier at the back. The evening would then be spent chasing the rabbits as they bolted from the decreasing rows of corn, since a rabbit caught in this way made for a good, free meal. This was before the days of myxomatosis which almost eradicated the rabbit population in England in the 1950s. Few country people could eat rabbit today, even a farmed one, for the memory of them dying in agony along the roadside is still too abhorrent.

In 1916, on the completion of Sandyhill farmhouse and outbuildings, Mr Akerman, who had been farming the land, moved from Mill Hill house. This enabled Mr George Freeman, who had been farming Mill Hill land, to move and relinquish the tenancy of Stones Farm to Mr Richard Stratton. Two extra farm names were now added to the estate register.

It was on Home Farm, in the early 1920s, that the first tractor appeared in the village. It was called 'Overtime' and was made in the United States in 1918 by the Waterloo Gasolene and Engine Co., Iowa, where it was called the 'Waterloo Boy'. It was a single-speed tractor with iron wheels (the two large rear wheels had diagonal iron bars across them), and was used with a left-hand cut McCormick binder. It was the pride and joy of Home Farm and Lionel Preston maintained it to perfection. It was still in use cultivating the land during the Second World War and ended its working days driving a hammer mill. John Deere & Co. exhibited a photograph of this 'Overtime' tractor on the January page of their 1989 calendar.

Previous reference has already been made to Mr Garne winning prizes for animals he exhibited at agricultural shows. These shows gave the farm workers an

Arch Jones seated on the Overtime tractor at Home Farm in the early 1920s.

incentive to take a greater interest in the animals they tended. Tremendous rivalry developed among the differing factions in Sherborne and the herdsmen and helpers could often be seen exercising their precious charges along the village roads.

Approaching show days the animals were groomed to perfection, loaded on to cattle floats drawn by two horses, and transported to Bourton-on-the-Water railway station where they were transferred to cattle trucks for the onward journey to favourite show venues such as the Royal Show, the Bull Ring at Birmingham, and the Gloucester Show and Sale. As the animals and their attendants would be away for several days, the carters returned home with their floats filled with coal or other provisions, perhaps stopping on the way at the Mousetrap Inn for a pint and some bread and cheese.

It was on such a return journey that Luke Preston, a carter from Home Farm, met with an accident that proved fatal when his hip was crushed. He was taken back to Bourton-on-the-Water hospital, where he died from his injuries.

The bulls, cows and heifers shown in the early years of the twentieth century were all pedigree shorthorns, which were much in demand in South America. In 1905 Home Farm took first prize for a shorthorn cow at Viscount Tredegar's Show, and in 1927 reserve champion for best shorthorn bull at the Three Counties Show (the three counties are Gloucestershire, Herefordshire and Worcestershire) and first prize for baby beef at Bourton-on-the-Water Christmas Fat Stock Show.

Winning show cards and rosettes were proudly displayed, nailed to the beams of the animal's feeding box or barn. Many such cards are still in evidence at Home Farm in the workshop and old cart shed, or in the barn.

Mr W. Tremaine's show bulls at Bourton-on-the-Water railway station in the early 1900s. Mr J. Saunders, the herdsman, is in the centre.

The poultrymen also had their day, winning first prize for dressed poultry at the United Hunts Lechlade Agricultural Show in 1923 (the United Hunts were Vale of White Horse, Cricklade, Old Berks, Earl Bathurst and Heythrop).

In 1928 Home Farm also won the best root exhibits with six turnips and six swedes, and took second place with their mangolds.

The Sherborne Farm herdsman, Jim Saunders, won many show prizes for shorthorns, and these were exhibited by W.H. Tremaine and Son.

Ernest Margetts, who worked on Stones Farm, was the proud possessor of a large, framed photograph of a group of five shorthorns which won a special prize as the best group of animals exhibited at the Birmingham Show in 1908. The animals had fascinating names: Fabulous Butterfly, Fairy Queen Butterfly, Prince Butterfly, First Butterfly and Master Butterfly. Their handlers were George Leach, Ernest Johnson (head herdsman), Mr Ash, Ernest Margetts and Fred Johnson – all worked for Mr George Freeman who was tenant farmer at that time.

The carters entered their horses in ploughing matches, usually two horses to a plough. The animals would be groomed until their coats shone, their manes and tails curry-combed, and the harnesses blacked and bedecked with gleaming brasses. The teams of horses would stretch right across a field, a real sight to behold. Arch Jones and Joe Moss, carters for Home Farm, regularly entered these competitions.

Around 1928, the estate was in financial difficulties due mainly to having to pay two lots of death duties within a year. Changes had to take place on Home Farm, which had been farmed mainly to supply the big house. Animals and equipment were sold off to raise capital.

Competitors lined up to compete in a ploughing match in the early 1920s.

Pigs belonging to Mr H. Tremaine at Northfield Barn sometime during the first half of this century.

The two large poultry houses at the Sheafhouse were the first to be closed down. While in operation, these houses, managed by Mr Harry Tyres and ably assisted by Evelyn Panter, each held 1,000 White Leghorn fowl. Each bird was tagged to enable a record to be kept of its laying capabilities, and as the birds entered the laying boxes they were trapped there until released by the egg collector, otherwise they were allowed to run freely in the field.

The next animals to go were the pigs, followed by the sheep and cattle. This resulted in the loss of many jobs. Fred Margetts, for example, one of the cattlemen unable to find alternative employment in the area, joined the RAF.

Mr Blake, tenant farmer at Home Farm, worked the farm for himself: however an agreement was drawn up whereby he would still supply Sherborne House with eggs and poultry, but this time on a commercial basis.

The unusual field names on farms in Sherborne are worth a mention. Space prohibits listing them all, however there are a few on Haycroft Farm in particular which are fascinating: Hungry Hill, Eggs Hill, Hand of Post Ground, Sideland, Thornhill, and Upper, Middle and Lower Bottom. Until the early part of the twentieth century there were two cottages across the fields from Haycroft Farm towards Grove Wood; the villagers called them Bittem Bottom. When the Sims family farmed at Haycroft during the 1930s, they referred to the cottages as being 'Up the Bottoms'.

The Sims family came to Haycroft Farm from Cornwall. Mr Sims, assisted by two of his sons, Godfrey and Everard, kept flocks of South Down and Oxford Down sheep. Their brief stay at the farm, only seven years before returning to Cornwall, broadened their outlook on farming and left them with many happy memories of the Cotswolds. So keen was their interest in sheep farming that they returned to the sheep sales at Andoversford from Cornwall on several occasions. On their farms in Cornwall, Everard kept pedigree Oxford Downs and Godfrey, Devon Longwool. These have now been crossed making a Devon/Cornwall breed.

The epitome of a farm yard prior to the Second World War, was a mixture of things: the sound of animals feeding and moving around in their stables, pens or boxes, a rick-yard full of thatched corn, hay ricks standing on staddle stones, a majestic Rhode Island Red cockerel with his harem of hens scratching around and a heap of steaming manure in the centre of the stock yard. In the surrounding fields, carters with teams of horses would be ploughing or sowing corn. Other men carting loads of manure to the fields in small horse-drawn tip carts to be emptied in heaps at spaced intervals, and distributed about the field with long handled and long tined forks, before ploughing into the soil.

Mr and Mrs Raikes were the tenants of Haycroft following the Sims family. Mr Raikes had been a member of the boat-race crew during his days at Oxford University. When they left Haycroft, the farm was sold to Mr Edward Hulton of the Hulton Publishing Company. This was the first of the Sherborne estate farms to be sold, followed by Broadmoor and Mill Hill Farm in more recent years.

Over the past sixty years many changes have taken place in agriculture, not only in farming methods, but also in the landscape. The most noticeable is the loss of so many lovely old ash, beech, chestnut, elm and oak trees. The extensive use of artificial herbicides and fertilizers has led to the virtual extinction of many wild shrubs and flowers, until legislation began to control their use. Hedges have been removed, making fields larger, and the old wooden five-bar gates have been replaced by wider, metal gates to accommodate the larger farm machines. Milking is now done in quantity by machinery, and rarely does the modern farmer milk a cow for personal consumption or set cream to make butter and cheese. Silage clamps, large plastic bags of silage and stacks of hay bales have replaced the hay rick.

The farm employee no longer has to negotiate a flight of worn stone steps, with no safety rail, carrying heavy sacks of corn on his back (a full Gopsil Brown sack of wheat weighed in at $2\frac{1}{4}$ cwts, while barley and oats weighed approximately 2 cwts), because heavy lifting is now done by forklift trucks. Corn, now gleaned, dried and stored in large silos, lofts or pits is transported loose, in large quantities, in huge lorries, with up to 25 tons moved at a time. Grazing animals are controlled in the pastures by electric fencing. Shorthorn cattle have been replaced by Friesians for their milk yield and Charollais, Limousin and Simmental bulls are coupled with Hereford, Aberdeen Angus, Limousin and Simmental cows which have been crossed with Friesians for beef production. Pigs are no longer reared on any of the Sherborne farms.

The latest method of crop farming is the 'set aside' scheme, whereby the farmer is paid £80 an acre, for a five-year term, not to sow the fields. The farmer is responsible for maintaining the hedges and ditches and, at least once a year, for mowing off 'rogue' crops. This scheme was introduced in order to cut down on the mountains of surplus grain that had built up during years of subsidized farming.

Haymaking in Mereslade in the early years of the century. The lady on the left in the dark dress is Mrs E. Johnson and in the white dress and dark hat is Mrs E. Robinson. The men on the wagon are Charlie and Clem Jones.

Most of the fields at Haycroft have been 'set aside', and are a sea of red poppies in the early summer.

Present-day farming is a very different and a solitary task for the combine driver. His only company, apart from his 'walkman' and CB radio, is the brief appearance of the tractor and corn trailer. The operation of unloading the corn from the combine is carried out while continuing the harvesting. Haymaking, too, is more lonely work than it was in the past with sophisticated machinery carrying out all but the most menial of tasks. This is quite a contrast to the scene pictured in an old photograph (probably taken during the First World War), where five men, five ladies (dressed in ankle-length dresses, wearing broad-brimmed and flower-trimmed hats), and three boys are raking and pitching hay up to two men (Charlie and Clem Jones) on a wagon drawn by two horses. It doesn't take much to imagine the chatter that accompanied that operation.

The changes have also brought considerable improvements to the living conditions of the farm workers: much higher rates of pay, four weeks' paid annual holiday and all bank holidays, and modernized cottages with all the accoutrements of modern life.

Those who worked the land were usually very dedicated to their occupation, remaining with their employer for the entirety of their working life. Long service awards and certificates were bestowed on the following individuals of Sherborne: Joseph Margetts in 1921 received a premium and certificate for working fifty years

Ernest Margetts receiving his long service medal from the Duke of Gloucester at the Three Counties Show in Hereford in 1954.

on Sherborne Farm for Mr W.H. Tremaine and Sons; his son Ernest was presented with an award by the late Duke of Gloucester, at the Three Counties Show in Hereford in 1954, for working Stones Farm for fifty-three years; Ernest's daughter, Sybil Longhurst, received her award at the Moreton-in-Marsh Show in 1987 for working as farm secretary for the Limbrick family for thirty-nine years; Lionel Preston, Jim Smith, and Cecil and Roland Harding, who worked Home Farm received their awards at the Three Counties Show; Albert and Peter Ash obtained their awards at the Royal Show at Stoneleigh in recognition of long service on Woeful Lake Farm.

Awards are still being won by the Sherborne farms in modern times, for example, Messrs W.H. and T.R. Limbrick of Home Farm won first prize for beef cattle in 1980. In 1987 they won reserve championship for winter barley, first prizes for winter barley, winter oats, two-year grass ley and big bales of silage; three second prizes for spring barley, winter barley and field beans, and third prize for beef cattle. Home Farm garden, tended by Mrs Celia Limbrick, won first prize for farm gardens in 1988.

The ploughing competitions continued in popularity, but the horses were gradually replaced by tractors. Cecil Vincent, tractor driver for W.H. Limbrick and Son on Stones Farm and latterly on Haycroft Farm won many prizes for ploughing a straight furrow. In recent years horse ploughing has reappeared at these ploughing competitions.

Messrs S.J. Phillips and Son, who farm Woeful Lake and other farms, still exhibit sheep. Tony Boucher has been shepherd at Woeful Lake and Aldsworth Farm for twenty years. His latest success was 'supreme champion' at the North Somerset Show with his Suffolk half-breed.

In January 1989, at an exhibition of paintings of agriculture held in the Mall Gallery in London, a painting which aroused considerable interest to viewers from the Cotswold area was of a 38 st. 11 lb pig bred and fed by Mr Gillett of Sherborne. This painting, attributed to John Miles of Northleach in 1820, was reproduced in the catalogue as *This Land is Our Land* and was put up for sale at a price of £38,000, by Stephen and Iona Joseph of Joseph Antiques. The question arose, 'Where did Mr Gillett live and farm?'. It has been established that a Gillett family farmed at Woeful Lake around that time. But to add to the confusion, a field on Sherborne Farm bears the name Gillett's Meadow.

Research in the Gloucester Records Office revealed that in 1857 an agreement was drawn up and witnessed by Lord Sherborne, Mr C. Gillett of Woeful Lake and Mr Mace of Sherborne Farm, decreeing that the fields named The Acre, Cowham and a further meadow on Sherborne Farm should be released to Mr Gillett, as Woeful Lake Farm was short of grazing land with sufficient water supply for the animals' needs. Over the years the venue of grazing land has been changed. Woeful Lake Farm now leases 80 acres of The Park from the estate. Mr C. Gillett was the son of the owner of the 'Fat Pig' and a brother to Mary who married Thomas Garne. As the Gilletts were a Quaker family, there is no record of their births or deaths in the parish register.

According to the *Victoria County History of Gloucestershire*, Woeful Lake probably derived its name from a 'woe' well, a name that indicated some calamity.

A painting of the 'Fat Pig' bred by Mr Gillett of Woeful Lake Farm, *c.* 1820. The artist was John Miles of Northleach, an itinerant painter of 'prize beasts'.

The well is no longer in use, but a tile with the inscription, 'Well' is to be found on the floor of the Woeful farmhouse kitchen.

Another illustration of the changes that have been brought about by modern farming techniques is in the number of employees now required for the day-to-day running of the farm: Home Farm is worked by the two tenant farmers, W.H. and T.R. Limbrick, and two employees; Sherborne and Sandyhill Farms, tenanted by W. and J. Tremaine, are worked with the assistance of five employees; Stones and Manor Farm at Windrush are tenanted by P. Summers and worked with the assistance of two employees.

The Cotswold sheep, which were plentiful in this area in days of old, almost became extinct. Their saviour was Mr Will Garne who farmed at Aldsworth, and held on to his flock for over thirty years. When he died, in 1967, his Cotswold flock was dispersed around the country.

CHAPTER FOUR

The Dutton Family of Sherborne

The Duttons, of Norman extraction, were descendants of Odard who crossed the Channel with William the Conqueror in 1066 and then settled in Duntune in Cheshire. From the sixteenth century, when Thomas bought the Manor, until the demise of the last Lord Sherborne in 1985, the Duttons remained lords of the manor. Their history has been one of prosperity and influence; at one time Lord Sherborne could ride from the Manor to Cheltenham without leaving his own lands – in all a distance of seventeen miles.

THE DUTTON DYNASTY

BORN		DIED
1507	Thomas Dutton	1581
1561	William Dutton, son of Thomas	1618
1594	John Dutton, son of William	1657
1640	William Dutton, nephew of John	1675
1642/6	Sir Ralph Dutton, brother of William	1721
1682	Sir John Dutton, son of Sir Ralph	1743
1712	Sir James Dutton, nephew of Sir John, changed his name from Lenox Naper when he inherited the estate	1776
1744	James Dutton, 1st Lord Sherborne, son of Sir James	1820
1779	John Dutton, 2nd Lord Sherborne, son of James	1862
1804	James Dutton, 3rd Lord Sherborne, son of John	1883
1831	Edward Dutton, 4th Lord Sherborne, son of James	1919
1840	Frederick Dutton, 5th Lord Sherborne, brother of Edward	1920
1873	James Dutton, 6th Lord Sherborne, nephew of Edward and Frederick	1949
1911	Charles Dutton, 7th Lord Sherborne, son of James	1982
1899	Ralph Dutton, 8th Lord Sherborne, cousin of Charles	1985

The Dutton family crest.

Thomas Dutton 1507–81

Thomas Dutton, formerly a student at Oxford and later surveyor of crown lands for Gloucestershire, bought the Manor of Sherborne in 1551 for the sum of £3,000 in six instalments of £500 plus £40 rent. It is likely that he obtained the money for the purchase from his wife of the time, a widow called Mrs Bigge who hailed from Westwell in Oxfordshire.

By his death in 1581 Thomas, who had been married three times, had extended his property in Sherborne and neighbouring villages to include:

in Sherborne – 40 messuages, 20 lofts, 20 cottages, 40 gardens, 2 dovecots, 3 water mills, 2,000 acres of land, 200 acres of meadow, 500 acres of pasture, 40 acres of woodland;

land in – Windridge (Windrush), Northlatch (Northleach), Bourton-on-the-Water, Wick Rissington, Brockhampton, Sevenhampton and Clapton.

Thomas also left 1,000 sheep in his will.

William Dutton 1561–1618

Thomas was succeeded by William, his son by his second wife Anne Kirton, daughter of a Merchant of the Staple at Calais. Like his father before him William set about acquiring lands, buying the Manor at Northleach in 1600 for £1,682 15s. 0d., Aldsworth in 1611, Standish in 1613 for £10,000, and founding a charity at Northleach. He was also responsible for the creation of a park from common pasture and open fields. His importance in the county was recognized when he was appointed Sheriff of Gloucestershire in 1590 and again in 1601.

By 1608, William had 27 servants (15 yeomen and 12 husbandmen) 2 of whom were shepherds. With a deep sense of his responsibilities and duties as a landowner William, in his will of 1618, made the following bequests to the poor:

I give for the benefit of the poor inhabitants of Northlache the inheritance of my house called commonly the great house and £200 in money which said house and stock of money I will have let and lent upon good security such as my heirs, The Bailiff of the town being the minister and four other of the most substantial inhabitants or most of them shall like of unto some honest tradesmen in Prestains or stuffs or in any such trade as may keep people from idleness by setting them to work.

John Dutton 1594–1657

John, the eldest surviving son of William, inherited the estate from his father in 1618. Of all the Duttons he was probably the most fascinating and influential. Certainly, he was a very wealthy man for his time and was acquainted with those from the highest echelons in the land. On his tomb he is described thus:

a person of a sharp Understanding/cleer Judgment, every way capable of those eminent services for his country which he Underwent as Knight of ye Shiere in several Parliaments and as Deputy Lieftenant. One who was Master of a large Fortune and owner of a mind Æquall to it. Noted for his great Hospitality farr and neer and his Charitable Relief of ye Poor.

John's many outside interests did not lead him to neglect his estate. Between 1651 and 1653 he had the manor house rebuilt, was granted a warrant to receive deer from, and to hunt in, Wychwood Forest, and he erected a hunting lodge and deer coursing run at Lodge Park in the south of the parish.

John Dutton was a passionate gambler, and the history books report that during one of his all-night sessions at a local inn he actually staked Sherborne estate, but on hearing the cry from the other gamblers 'Sherborne's up', his everpresent man-servant removed him bodily from the table and took him home. Contrary to his gambling fetish, John was very wary of expending money needlessly: he was imprisoned twice for refusing to pay ship money and was fined on two occasions; the first for £3,434 and the second for £1,782, for undervaluing his estates to that amount.

Despite these problems he was created Deputy Lieutenant of the County, which he represented in the Parliaments of 1624, 1625 and 1640. At this time he was a staunch Royalist, commenting to Sir Robert Cooke that he would: 'Never more trust any man that wore his hayre shorter than his ears'.

Despite his deformity (he was probably a hunchback), John Dutton, nicknamed 'Crump Dutton', became a colonel in the Royalist army and took an active part in the siege of Gloucester, after which he was discharged due to his disability.

John was later to play a major part in the drawing up of Articles for the Treaty of Surrender at Oxford. It is obvious that at some point he underwent a complete change in his political allegiances, for not only did he become a keen Parliamentarian, he even went so far as to disinherit his daughters for refusing to change their monarchist views.

How and when he became a personal friend of Oliver Cromwell is unclear but by 27 December 1655, Cromwell was writing to the Committee of Sequestrations:

> Gentlemen, I have understood that you have sent to Mr John Dutton of Sherborne for a perticuler of his Estate in pursuance of yor instructions. These are to let you know that the Gentleman hath given so many reall Testimonys of his affection to the Government and to my person in particular, so constantly for many years last past, that noe man yt I knowe of in England, hath done more wch is a thing knowne both to myselfe and diverse of the Council and therefore as I could have wisht that I had knowne he had had any estate in yore Countrye, before you had sent to hym. Soe now i doe desire you to forbeare the sendinge any further to hym, or of gieveing to you or his estate any further disturbance whatsoever. In assurance of your confirmitye here to I rest
>
> Yor loveinge Friend,
> Whitehall   'Oliver P'
>   27th Decr, 1655.

See also a letter from Oliver Cromwell to his Chief Ranger, referring to John Dutton (opposite).

When John Dutton died in 1657, he left instructions to his friend Cromwell in his will:

> My will and humble request and desire unto his Highness the Lord Protector is that His Highness will be pleased to take upon him the guardianship and disposing of my nephew William Dutton and of that estate I have left unto him which by my Deed of Settlement and this my Will may appear. And that His Highness would be pleased in order to my former desires I according to the discourse that has passed betwixt us thereupon that when he shall come to ripeness of age (If it shall so please God) a marriage may be had betwixt my said nephew William Dutton and the Lady Frances Cromwell His Highness' youngest daughter, which I much desire and (if it takes effect) shall account it as a blessing from God.

John was buried at Sherborne on 28 February 1657. His ghost is said to haunt some parts of the village and Lodge Park to this day.

William Dutton 1640–75

William, the son of John Dutton's brother Sir Ralph, succeeded his uncle to the estate of Sherborne in 1657. As his uncle had requested he lived in the Cromwell household from 1653, staying with the family at Hampton Court and attending school at Eton. He did not, however, marry Frances Cromwell. In 1657 she married a Mr Rich who died just three months later. Frances went on to marry Sir John Russell and lived to the ripe old age of eighty-two. William Dutton married Mary, daughter of Viscount Scudamore and widow of Thomas Russell. He died in 1675 without issue.

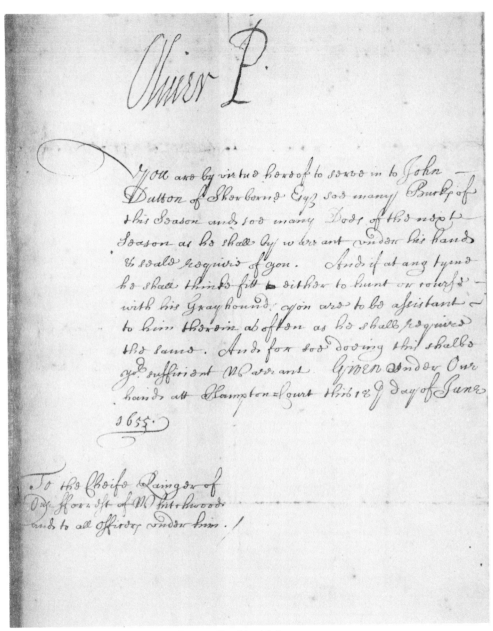

Translation of a letter from Oliver Cromwell to his chief ranger:
  You are by virtue hereof to send in to John Dutton of Sherborne Esq so many Bucks of this season and so many Does of the next season as he shall by warrant under his hand should require of you. And if at any time he shall think fit either to hunt or roust with his greyhounds, you are to be assistant to him therein as often as he shall require the same. And for so doing this shall be your sufficient warrant. Given under our hands at Hampton Court this 18th day of June 1655.
          To the Chief Ranger of our Forest of Whichwood and to all Officers under him.

Sir Ralph Dutton 1642/6–1721

William was succeeded by his brother Ralph, an inveterate gambler, who was created a baronet by patent on 20 June 1678. Ralph appeared to have considerable problems in controlling the management of his estate and monies as the following indenture (one of many) illustrates:

Indenture of assignment
23 June 1708

between Sir Phillip Meadows, of St Anne's Westminster, Knight, of the one part and Hans Sloane, of St Giles-in-the-Field, M.D. and Richard Husbands of St Andrews, Holborn, Gent of the other part by which Sir Ralph Dutton for £600 to Sloane and Husbands for £270 each. Signed by Phillip Meadows with his receipt for the money.

By 1709 it had become necessary for Ralph's son, John, to take over control of the estate. An indenture of assignment dated 4 February 1709–10 between the Right Worshipful Sir Ralph Dutton of Sherborne, Bart. and John Dutton Esq., his son and heir, says that: 'Sir Ralph assigns to the said John the whole of his real and personal estate in return for £5,000 and a life annuity of £400 yearly.'

In a later deed John also: 'undertakes to satisfy all debts that Dame Mary (his mother) may contract and provide her and her daughters with maintenance and to indemnify Sir Ralph from all debts due by him to Dr Barwick and John Prinn'.

During this time at least one member of the family fancied herself as a 'poet'. In 1711 Jane Dutton wrote the following epistle to her sister:

> Dear Sister, I am grown a poet
> So here's a specimen to show it,
> Poor Lady Talbot's Ockey's dead
> And with him all her joys are fled,
> You cannot blame a grief so great
> As sure no dog was e'er so sweet.
> For beauty, sense and love sincere,
> He beats all dogs in Gloucestershire.
> Pray then learn from what's above
> The fate attending dogs we love.
> I have said enough, so must conclude my letter
> And am sorry I can't write better.

Sir John Dutton 1682–1743

Sir John Dutton took control of the estate from his father in 1709. He was twice married, first to Mary, daughter of Sir Rushout Cullen, and secondly to Mary, daughter of Francis Keck of Great Tew in Oxfordshire.

He died in 1743 without issue and left the estates to his sister Anne's son, James Lenox Naper.

Sir John was a prodigious and meticulous record keeper. Some fascinating details of his life can be followed through his accounts records:

1723	Two journeys of teams to Woodstock to fetch chimney pieces and hearth stone for the new parlour, drawing room and study	6s. 0d.
	To Mr Collivoe for his journey from London to view my pictures in order to mend them	£6 6s. 0d.
	A wrought iron bed for my sister's room	£43 9s. 0d.
	For Dutch table linen	£50 9s. 3d.
	For a Bob-Peroke [wig]	£3 0s. 6d.
1725	The Cheltenham drummer's Christmas box	2s. 6d.
	A large Yew tree for the gardens	£1 5s. 0d.
	A tied up peruke	£6 6s. 0d.
	To the bell ringers at Standish	13s. 0d.
	To Signr. Vassalli for making fourteen busts and pedestalls for my hall	£20 9s. 0d.
	100 honeysuckles and 100 sweet briars	£1 13s. 4d.
	700 witch elms for the gardens	£7 10s. 0d.
1726	Sash for my nightgown [evening suit]	8s. 0d.
	To Mr Dahl for painting my picture at 3/4 length	£15 15s. 0d.
	For cleaning the monuments in the Church	£37 3s. 0d.
1727	37 yards of calico at 8s. per yard	£16 16s. 0d.
	For a mourning sword and buckles	15s. 6d.
	For a long wig for myself	£6 6s. 0d.
	For a mourning suit for the King, waistcoat lined with silk	£9 12s. 0d.
	Weather glass	6s. 0d.
1728	Gold repeating watch and chain for a present for Mr Keck	£84 0s. 0d.
	Settlement on Mrs Keck	£21 0s. 0d.
	His clerk	£7 17s. 6d.
	Spent showing my sister Hampton Court	£1 4s. 0d.
	Spent showing my sister Clarement and My Lord Lincoln's and expenses with horse	£1 7s. 0d.
	For a seal for Mrs Keck	£4 4s. 0d.
	For her wedding ring	15s. 0d.
	To the Bishop of Ely marrying of me (1st June)	£10 10s. 0d.
	To his Chaplain and servants	£4 0s. 6d.
	To the bells and music at Hampstead	£5 5s. 0d.
	A pair of diamond earrings for my wife	£350 0s. 0d.
	51 lbs of tea, Imperial and Bohea	£4 16s. 6d.
	New coach with springs, lined with cafoy, gilt and painted with mosaic work	£145 9s. 0d.

Sir John's marriage to Mary Keck was destined to be a short one. In 1729 he made a trip and recorded:

Expenses on the road with my wife going to London

With two coaches four days	£17 8s. 1d.
For a sequel to the *Beggar's Opera*	2s. 6d.
For a peruke (wig)	£7 2s. 0d.
Orange flower water	5s. 0d.
To a curate and clerk of St James's Parish for baptising 'my child privately' (5th June)	15s. 6d.
Servant's expenses 'attending my wife and child's corpse' into the country	£3 5s. 0d.
Medical attendance	£53 12s. 0d.
To the midwife	30 guineas
Undertaker	£76 0s. 0d.
Four Flambeaux to light the vault	4s. 0d.
St. James's Parish Church fees for the funeral	£1 6s. 0d.
To late wife's nurse instead of a sheet she claimed on her death	£1 1s. 0d.

By 1730 the death of his wife was still costing Sir John:

For the use of a Mourning Coach a year and threequarters for my father, Keck and my late wife	£37 0s. 0d.

But dealing with more mundane matters was still the responsibility of the baronet:

For an apron to Charlott Budget	8s. 5d.
13 hounds, a gift from the Duke of Bolton	
A drench for a mad dog	1s. 4d.
And liver wart for the same	2s. 0d.

1731	A coach and six horses bringing me from Parliament	£7 0s. 0d.
	To the Attorney General for his opinion concerning the £5,000 of my first wife's jointure, which was to be paid to me after Sir Rushout Cullen's death which sum I lost through Lord Letchmere's negligence in drawing the writings	£3 5s. 6d.
1732	For exchange of my old coach for a new chariot machine	£35 0s. 0d.
	To Mrs Kyle for ticking and strapping to mend the umbrellas in my room	4s. 3d.
	For a tin cover for my sundial	6s. 0d.
	Five hogs heads of port	£105 12s. 0d.
1733	Five dozen garden pots for orange trees	£3 0s. 0d.
	Three hogs heads of Mountain white wine	£45 0s. 0d.
	To ye musick at Mead Mowing	1s. 0d.
	Making serpentine walks behind the lodge	£4 15s. 9d.
	To Mr Whitworth for 25 oaks from Wychwood Forest	£16 18s. 0d.
	Green cloth for liveries	£9 0s. 0d.
	Killing a polecat in the pigeon house	1s. 0d.
	For two brass plates for Inigo Jones's pictures	1s. 9d.
	Two suits of ribbons a present to Mrs Kemeys	3s. 0d.

Sir James Dutton 1712–76

When Sir John died in 1743 his nephew James Lenox Naper inherited Sherborne. A stipulation for this inheritance was that he change his name to Dutton.

Like many of his forebears, as Lord of the Manor, James held high office in the county. In 1758 he was Deputy Lieutenant of Gloucestershire. In 1772 he made his will thus:

> To my dear wife Jane 1,000 guineas to be paid within three months, also my coach and post chaire, harness and all horses thereto belonging and six milch cows, my crops of oats and one of my best ricks of hay to her sole use, with the use of her personal effects and an Annuity of £1,200 for her life in lieu of Dower.

James also bequeathed charitable donations in the locality:

> To Gloucester Infirmary £200
> To the poor of Sherborne and Northleach £20
> To the poor of Eastington, Aldsworth and Windrush £10

His son James was made sole executor of the will and was earnestly recommended to complete the improvements to his house and lands.

Due to a doubt as to his son's attentiveness in carrying out these wishes, Sir James amended his will in 1776, bequeathing £10,600 to Henry, Duke of Beaufort in trust:

> to lay out and expend the same upon the Testator's intended enclosure of the Manor of Sherborne and the completion of my house at Sherborne upon the plan that I will leave for that purpose.

James Dutton (1st Lord Sherborne) 1774–1820

James Dutton, like his father before him, was Sheriff of Gloucestershire. He was married in 1774 to Elizabeth Coke of Derby. She brought with her a dowry of an estate, valued at £11,070, in Hillingdon, Middlesex, plus property in Westminster.

On 20 May 1784 James was created the 1st Baron of Sherborne by George III's original Patent of Peerage. The new Lord Sherborne found the costs associated with the acquisition of his title to be quite high. The baron's robe itself cost £27 10s. and the following accounts, found among the general muniments, show the fees paid in passing the Patent:

Secretary of State's Office	£32 8s. 6d.
Attorney General	£39 0s. 0d.
Signet Office	£12 3s. 6d.
Privy Seal Office	£14 3s. 6d.
Crown Office	£251 16s. 0d.

Sherborne House dining room photographed in 1877.

Writ of Summons	£2 2s. 0d.
Deputy Gazette Writer	£1 1s. 0d.
Passing the Patent	£21 0s. 0d.
	£373 14s. 6d.

He also paid 3 guineas to distribute among the yeomen, watersmen and the 'Gentleman Porters at the Queen's House' and £108 10s. 6d. to the Herald's College.

Lord Sherborne, taking a leaf from his father's book, also left a series of fascinating accounts. James's valet, John Villar, recorded the following expenses:

2 Jan. 1776	To the man that did play for Mistresse's welcome to Bath	10s. 6d.
9 May 1777	Gave the Morrice dancers	10s. 0d.
1778	Sending letters by the bell men [men who went round with a bell just prior to the departure of the post]	1d.
	For a chair to go to church	2s. 0d.

1781 Mistress treating John to the Play	2s. 0d.
Bottle of Essence of Bergamot (a popular perfume)	2s. 0d.
1782 For turnpikes for going to Kensington to buy a nosegay for Mistress	2d.
For coach hire at one of Mr Bannister's benefits [T. Bannister the comedian]	1s. 6d.
1784 To 12 tickets for Drury Lane Playhouse at ½ price	30s. 0d.
To 6 box tickets for Covent Garden	30s. 0d.
1785 To 6 lbs of Orange Bloom powder for Lady Sherborne	15s. 0d.
To a man that charmed the warts away	2s. 0d.
To the Harper at Bangor Ferry	1s. 0d.
1786 To the carriage of my Lady's stick from Shrewsbury to Cirencester	2s. 10d.
To 2 fiddlers from Stow	10s. 6d.
To Mr Hall for waiting the time that the Duke and Duchess of Beaufort were at Sherborne	2s. 0d.
1791 To two sets of Mummers at Sherborne	7s. 6d.
1792 Richard the Fiddler for two days coming over to Sherborne but did not play to the Ladies	4s. 0d.
1795 Paid David for a Hackney Coach called for when in London, when Lady Sherborne's coach wheel broke	1s. 0d.

Lord Sherborne died in 1820 and was buried, as specified in his will, in a coffin covered with crimson silk velvet adorned with 'Glory and Urn, 12 cherubs and 3,000 brass nails'. Black hangings adorned the church. All in all the funeral expenses came to over £500.

John Dutton (2nd Lord Sherborne) 1779–1862

John, who had married the Hon. Mary Legge in 1803, succeeded his father to the title and lands in 1820. However, he did not take his seat in the House of Lords until 1 October 1830.

For twenty years he was President of the Council of Cheltenham College (for boys) which was founded in 1841 and he provided much of the money for building Holy Trinity church.

John was also responsible for rebuilding Sherborne House (in a style much akin to its present format). It is recorded that, during the reconstruction, the books and family papers were given into the safekeeping of the Vicar of Windrush and Sherborne. This proved to be a disastrous choice as the old gentleman, somewhat careless in his housekeeping, instructed a servant to dispose of them all. Many fine, black leather folios and ancient parchments found their way into the hands of the local shoemaker, who cut them up for boots and shoes. It wasn't until nearly thirty years later that the remnants were discovered and returned to Sherborne House.

By this time Lord Sherborne was a man of considerable wealth, and in addition to his lands in and around Sherborne he owned estates in Great Rissington, Coln St Aldwyns, Standish, Randwick, Moreton Valence, Stonehouse, Haresfield and Bibury.

During his lifetime John attended two coronations. On 8 Septebmer 1831, for the coronation of William IV, he arose at 5 a.m., departed Sherborne at 7.30 a.m. and did not return until after 6 p.m. For the coronation of Queen Victoria, on 28 June 1838, Lord and Lady Sherborne watched the royal procession from the home of Lady de la Zouche.

On 19 October 1862, at 3 o'clock in the afternoon, John 'passed away without pain'. He was buried on 27 October and was succeeded by his son James.

James Dutton (3rd Lord Sherborne) 1804–83

James Dutton became the 3rd Lord Sherborne, on the death of his father in 1862, until his demise in 1883. During his era the present-day school at Sherborne was built. James had many photographs taken of both the interior and exterior of the house, when photography was in its infancy.

Under his employ was an indoor staff of 23 (14 females and 9 males), together with 11 senior outdoor staff.

Edward Dutton (4th Lord Sherborne) 1831–1919

A letter from Lord Sherborne to his fiancée, Miss Emily de Stern, written 13 July 1891:

> My Dearest,
> I distinctly said at my last interview that I should not call again until you name the day. I will not call tomorrow because if I call and you do not name the day I shall leave the house and never speak to you again, therefore it is only fair to warn you.
> Yours sincerely,
Sherborne.

They were eventually married in 1893 when he was sixty two years old.

According to *Kelly's Directory* of 1910, Edward Dutton's agent was Robert Gray of The Cottage, Sherborne. The tenant farmers at this time were:

Albert Akerman, Sandyhill Farm
Frank Blake, Home Farm (farm bailiff)
Richard Hicks, Woeful Lake Farm
George Freeman, Stones Farm
Charles Jeffries, Broadmoor Farm
Robert Singer, Haycroft Farm
William Tremaine, Sherborne Farm.

In the village there was a carrier, a haulier, a sub-postmaster, a baker, a

The 3rd Lord Sherborne who was responsible for the building of the present school.

Sherborne House senior outdoor staff in the 1920s. Centre back row is Mr J. Taylor and on his left is Mr H. Taylor. Seated on the extreme right is Mr T. Mathews.

blacksmith, a wheelwright and carpenter, three shopkeepers, a schoolmaster and a schoolmistress. The total weekly wage on the estate at this time was £72 18s. 3d. The highest paid employee was the head-keeper at £1 15s. 9d., while the majority received between 15s. and 18s. per week.

Frederick (5th Lord Sherborne) 1840–1920

Edward was succeeded in July 1919 by his brother the Revd Frederick Dutton, who was Vicar of Sherborne from 1870–4 and of Bibury from 1874–1916.

His baronetcy was short lived, since he died on 2 January 1920.

James (6th Lord Sherborne) 1873–1949

James Huntley was the nephew of Edward and Frederick. He was a military man with a reputation for being blunt. He also served as a justice of the peace.

During the Second World War he vacated Sherborne House (while the house was taken over by the armed forces) and settled in the Manor House at Windrush.

James was a keen angler and formed a shooting syndicate with his friend Sir Alan Anderson.

Lord Sherborne and his wife, Lady Ethel, had four children, two sons, Charles and George, and two daughters, Pamela and Juliet. The Hon. George, more interested in village affairs than his brother, enjoyed chatting with the villagers. He attempted several business ventures, including duck farming and mushroom growing, and he also worked for a short time in the Norwegian Embassy during

Sherborne House indoor staff photographed in 1877.

which time, it is remembered, he brought a ravishing Norwegian lady friend to Sherborne House.

Both brothers were members of the ATA (Air Transport Auxiliary) during the war. During a trip to Turkey, George was arrested and spent several days in gaol. He spent the later years of his life, with his wife, managing a hotel near Hereford.

The two daughters were very different in disposition: Pamela was an extrovert and worked in London, while Juliet was very shy and reserved.

As a child Juliet did not enjoy good health, spending much time in Switzerland accompanied by her governess, however, she was an excellent horsewoman. During haymaking and harvest she liked to join the workers on Home Farm and would lead the horses while the wagons were being loaded with hay or sheaves of corn. Juliet had a little donkey cart, with a specially made trap door in the back to enable her dogs to jump in. She was always attended by her governess who would take along her knitting to while away the hours. A hamper containing their meal, which was consumed a discreet distance away from the workers, was placed in the cart. Their constant presence proved at times to be an irritation to the farm employees.

During the war years Juliet continued to 'help out' on the farm, but her great love was for her dogs; she left the proceeds from the sale of her house, Windrush Manor, to the League for Canine Refuge.

Moving old coaches from the stable yard at Sherborne House to make room for occupation by army personnel in 1940. Left to right: W. Hall (chauffeur), Hon. Charles Dutton, J. Meadwell (under chauffeur), S. Mosson (groom).

None of the Sherborne offspring gave issue, in fact neither of the daughters married.

Following the death of Edward Dutton, and his brother Frederick a year later, heavy death duties were to take their toll on the estate, resulting in labour reductions. The first to be affected was Home Farm. According to *Kelly's Directory* of 1927, Mr Robert Gray remained as the estate agent with Walter Rowe as assistant overseer. The parish clerk was Jack Saunders. The tenant farmers were as follows:

Albert Akerman, Sandy Hill
Frank Blake, Home Farm
Aubrey Handy, Haycroft (breeding pure Percherons)
Richard Houlton, Mill Hill
William Ing, Woeful Lake (he was the first man in Sherborne to own a motor car and his phone number was Sherborne 1)
Alexander Lockart, Broadmoor
Richard F. Stratton, Stones
William Tremaine, Sherborne.

The following is a list of other notable artisans in Sherborne at that time:

head forester, Thomas Dow of Waterloo Cottage
postmaster, Frederick Townsend
carrier, Francis D. Lester
shopkeeper, Albert Townsend (at the post office)
shopkeeper, Sarah Drinkwater (at No. 54 Sherborne)
gamekeeper, Alan Hill
haulier, Charles Jones
head gardener, Arthur Mitchell
wheelwright, William Scregg
manager of the poultry farm at the Sheafhouse, William H. Tyres, assisted by Evelyn Panter.

The village had by now lost both its baker and blacksmith.

To commemorate Miss Juliet Dutton's twenty-first birthday, lamp-posts holding oil lamps were erected at strategic points along the village street, but the distances between them were so great that they did not serve any real purpose. They were eventually abandoned and the posts were removed, with the exception of the one adjacent to the war memorial.

The Right Honourable James Dutton died in 1949 and was buried in the Sherborne vault.

Charles (7th Lord Sherborne) 1911–82

Charles, the eldest son of James, was born in 1911 and was educated at Stowe School. He was very shy and reserved with strangers, but generous to his friends and had a great sense of humour. During the Second World War, despite losing his right arm as a result of a rugby accident, he was an ATA pilot. His main task was to

Haymaking on Home Farm in the late 1920s. Juliet Dutton is leading the horses and Winnie George is behind.

Charles Dutton, the 7th Lord Sherborne.

ferry aircraft and he often brought one into Little Rissington Maintenance Unit for repairs. Eventually, Charles became CO of the ATA unit at White Waltham.

In March 1943, Charles married Mrs Jenkinson, née Miss Joan Molesworth Dunn, daughter of Sir James Dunn.

Charles died without issue on Christmas Day 1982. He left over £7 million gross. The bulk of his estate, which included 500 acres of woodland, an extensive acreage of farmland, an Iron Age earthwork, Windrush Camp, and parts of the villages of Sherborne, Windrush and Aldsworth, was left to the National Trust. The National Trust plan to restore Lodge Park, where Charles and his wife resided, to its original splendour.

Ralph (8th Lord Sherborne) 1899–1985

Ralph succeeded his cousin Charles in title only. He was in residence in Hinton Amner House, Arlesford, Hampshire. At the age of eighty-six, Ralph died, three years after Charles on 22 April 1985, without issuse.

There being no near male relatives, Ralph's death brought the dynasty to an end as had been predicted by a supposed curse inflicted on the family by the Abbots of

Lady Joan Sherborne.

Winchcombe in the seventeenth-century. This curse was said to have been put on the Dutton family when 'Crump' Dutton had the site of the church moved by 10 feet to accommodate his plans for the rebuilding of the house during the 1650s.

The National Trust had by this time taken over the running of the estate, preserving the individual character of the village. They took full control on 1 January 1989.

CHAPTER FIVE

Sherborne House

The original Sherborne House was thought to have been built on the site of a St Mary's monastery. Despite being rebuilt in the seventeenth century and again in the nineteenth century, Sherborne House has always retained a position of prominence midway between the two halves of the village.

The first house was built, between 1651 and 1653, on the orders of a Mr John Dutton. He employed a local master builder, Valentine Strong of Taynton, Oxfordshire, who was also the architect. An artist's impression, from 1768, shows the west elevation having two large wings, but these no longer exist. A stable block was added in 1776.

In the 1830s the house was rebuilt, mainly in a nineteenth-century Renaissance style. The older building was carefully dismantled, with each of the stones being numbered for reincorporation into the new building. When the new building was completed, Lord Sherborne was dissatisfied with the work and ordered extensive alterations, to be carried out at the expense of the architect.

Traces of the original house may still be found in some parts of the modern house.

South view of Sherborne House photographed in 1877.

The house, with over one hundred rooms, was said to have had a window for each day of the year.

Mrs Marjorie Mate recalls that the front seats in the church were reserved for the Dutton family who entered by the vestry door. The service did not begin until they were seated, even if late.

Sherborne House, home to the Dutton family until the middle of the twentieth century, was the seat of the lord of the manor. At the start of the Second World War, when the Duttons moved to smaller premises, namely the Windrush Manor and Lodge Park near Aldsworth, the house was taken over by units of the British and American armies.

Then from 1947, until 1966, Sherborne House was the home to Kings School, a private school for boys with Mr Mosey as headmaster.

For five years the house remained empty until, in 1970, it was bought to be used by the Foundation of the International Academy for Continuous Education, with Mr Bennett as principal.

A few years later a religious group called the Beshara Trust took up residence and in 1981, the house was sold to a company for conversion into luxury apartments.

LODGE PARK

Lodge Park, situated in the south-west of Sherborne parish, was built in the seventeenth century as a hunting lodge for John (Crump) Dutton.

An ashlar building with rusticated quoins, mullioned windows and a balustraded

Lodge Park, now in the hands of the National Trust who hope to restore it to its original appearance, and open it to the public.

parapet, Lodge Park is constructed in the style of Inigo Jones although it is more likely to have been designed by his pupil, John Webb. The square outline bears a similarity to Lambert Hall in Northamptonshire, another of John Webb's designs. Valentine Strong, designer and constructor of Sherborne House, was also responsible for the construction of Lodge Park.

Originally, the interior comprised two large rooms, one of which was a banqueting hall. It also provided a broad balcony, and from the leads of the roof the ladies and gentlemen were able to follow the sport of deer coursing. A spinney, from which the 'slipper' released the deer and greyhounds, can still be seen – as can the run which lies to the west of the Lodge Park road.

Immediately in front of the Lodge was a paddock, a mile in length, where the coursing took place. To test their speed the deer were allowed to escape through an aperture, at the end of the course, which was quickly closed by an attendant to prevent the greyhound following.

A quote taken from *A Survey of Twenty-Six Counties*, 1634, written by 'a lieutenant, accompanied by a captain and an ancient', gave evidence of the beauty of the setting;

> My afternoon's travell presented to my Eye many more places and seats of Noble Knights and Worthy Gentlemen . . . but more especially one stately, rich, compacted building all of Free stone, flat and cover'd with lead, with

Sherborne House senior outdoor staff photographed in 1877. Extreme left is Mr Evans (Gamekeeper) and in the back row, fourth from left, is Mr Sly (Carpenter). Others in the photograph are: Messrs Hodges, Scott, Guy, James, Robinson, Haynes, Mumford, Bunting and Old Bunting.

strong battlements about not much unlike to that goodly and magnificent building, the Banqueting House at Whitehall . . . . This stately Lodge was lately built at the great cost, and charges of a noble and true hearted gentlemen, more for the pleasure of his worthy friends, than to his own profit. It is richly furnished to entertaine them to see the Kingly sport, and pleasure, admirably performed, in that rare Paddock course of a mile in length, and wall'd on either side. There I spent a full houre, with the good favour of the keeper, in viewing that neat, rare building, the rich furnish'd rooms, the hansome contriv'd Pens and Places, where the Deere are kept and turn'd out for the Course, all the manner, and order of the Paddock Sport.

According to an inventory, dated 1740, the Lodge was still in use when the dining room was re-equipped with: 'Two Marble slabs and Frames, two Settees, Fan Stools and six colloms'.

With the demise of deer coursing, fox hunting became the replacement sport. In December 1748, the *London Evening Post* printed a report of the combined Chedworth and Sherborne hounds chasing the fox.

In 1890 the Lodge was used as two gamekeeper's cottages but, by the end of the nineteenth century, Lady Emma Sherborne had it converted into a dwelling house with an extension to the rear.

Entrance to the renovated ice house, in the Pleasure Ground wood of Sherborne House, photographed in 1990.

A circular staircase was later installed and, at the end of the drive leading from the Park road, ornate iron gates with two small lodges were erected. The grounds in front of the lodge were then laid out. The 7th Lord Sherborne, Charles Dutton, and his wife, used it as their home until his death in 1982.

In the yard directly behind Sherborne House stands an octagonal-shaped butter house which may have been reconstructed from an even older dovecote. During the early part of this century it was used for hanging the slaughtered carcases of sheep and pigs reared on Home Farm. Its present use is an electrical sub-station for the House.

Two relics of the opulent life of the Dutton family are to be found in the heart of the Pleasure Ground wood situated on the South side of the House. One is an old wrought iron seat standing on a concrete base, (both completely surrounding an old Yew tree), which the National Trust are having restored. The second is an old ice house which was completely restored in 1988 by Leslie and David Hayward.

Several cut stone pillar gateways are still to be found as evidence of the rides used by the gentry through this wood which in the Spring is a mass of aconites, snowdrops and daffodils.

On Sunday 1st March 1990 the National Trust officially opened the first of their walks incorporating this wood. Between sixty and seventy people took part finishing up in the Social Club for cups of tea and home-made cakes.

Leading the walk was Mr Pearce head of this National Trust region, also present were Andrew Langton, Land Agent and Andrew Maylead, village warden.

CHAPTER SIX

Sherborne Church

The present church, which is dedicated to Mary Magdalene, stands adjacent to Sherborne House in the centre of the village.

Although of mainly nineteenth-century construction, part of a fourteenth-century tower still stands, although with the later addition of a steeple and vaulted roof.

The belfry contains six bells, the fourth of which has been rung for over six hundred years. A separate Dutton family vault stands, in the old cemetery, at the west end of the stable block alongside the church. Folklore reputes that a 'white lady' emerges from the vault, at night, and rolls a huge boulder down to the brook.

A number of monuments to the Dutton family can be seen within the church: between black marble columns and standing shrouded in a niche is the figure of John Dutton of 1656; Sir John Dutton of 1742, sculptured by Rysbrack, is resplendent in Roman costume; an eighteenth-century sculpture depicts an angel trampling the skeleton of death.

Sherborne Church choir in 1913.

Interior of Sherborne Church photographed in 1877.

In the *Victoria County History of Sherborne* there is mention of 'the chapel of St John', which existed in the thirteenth century. Described as the 'West End Chapel' in 1549, it was included, with its two bells, in a grant by the crown. Villagers in the past mentioned that the site of this chapel was along the Farmington road, immediately after Haycroft Farm, and the small wood to the right was known as 'Cemetery Copse'.

There was one recusant in Sherborne in 1577, but there is no other known record of any Nonconformists.

In 1776 the two vicarages of Windrush and Sherborne were united, and the benefice was valued then at £100 per annum. Both the vicar and curate lived in Northleach. In 1825 the curate was resident in Windrush, while the vicar lived a distance of fifty miles away, but since 1840 the vicar has resided in Windrush.

On 26 May 1837, a letter, relating to the Sherborne churchyard, was received from the Church Commissioners accepting a piece of land additional to the burial ground of Sherborne church. A plan of the ground and part elevation of the church was included.

At the beginning of the twentieth century, the original pews were removed from the church. Replacements, from a redundant church in Gloucester, have recently been purchased and some, donated by village folk, now bear inscribed plaques in memory of loved ones.

The church was reroofed and renovated in 1989/90 by local builders, Mustoe and Sons of Northleach. On 11 February 1990 a thanksgiving service was held, conducted by the parish vicar the Revd Colin McCarter in the presence of Archdeacon the Venerable John Lewis, to celebrate the completion of the work.

Unveiling of the War Memorial in 1926.

The war memorial with the school in background. Note the motorcycle and side-car in the foreground.

To honour the occasion all six bells were rung, a very rare occurrence indeed, by the following bell-ringers: Brian Hall and Bert Phipps of Windrush; Lew Sly from Northleach and three others from Burford. Mrs Cathie Hall played the organ. The service was followed by glasses of wine, served by the church councillors.

The War Memorial

The village war memorial, situated near the post office, bears the names of the local men who lost their lives during the First and Second World Wars.

Designed in Clipsham stone, the monument was made and erected by Alfred Groves of Shipton under Wychwood, at a cost of £117 15s. 0d. and was unveiled on 12th of November 1926 by Lord Sherborne, following a service in the church.

The following is the total account for the monument:

A. Groves account:
To Memorial as plan ....£100 0s. 0d.
To extra 5 doz. letters in inscription ....£1 5s. 0d.
To extra laying, paving and hauling from Huntsmans Quarry £16 10s. 0d.

£117 15s. 0d.

Sherborne Church choir in 1926. Back row, left to right: Leslie Joy, Fred Dadge (organist), Mr Goddard, Mr Dow. Third row: Dick Renn, Fred Stevens, Charlie Jones (jun.), Bill Petrie, Mr E. Panter, Harry Tyres, Teddy Williams. Second row: Billy Hill, Ivor Larner, Ron Walker, Revd George Warner, Alfred Margetts, Wilf Tyres, Francis Larner. Front row: Teddy Margetts, Freddy Turner, Ernie Larner, Reg Cyphus, Lionel Cyphus, Ronald Hicks.

To Estate labour walling on site....................................... £40 6s. 2d.
To A. Groves & Sons, Supplying and erecting .... £117 15s. 0d.
To J.E. Thorpes, Architect's fees....................................£15 15s. 0d.

£173 16s. 2d.

Lord Sherborne met further costs required for the following site preparation: removing the soil; supplying and laying drainage pipes (George Rainbow was in charge of these tasks and E. Souls, A. Margetts, L. Lester, F. Large, C. Large, A. Cyphus, J. Dixon, F. Souls, A. Moss and L. Hemming provided the labour). Supplying stone for the surrounding wall and hauling wallstone from the quarry at Catts Abbey and gravel from the pits on the common was the job of Charlie Jones at a cost of £7 2s. 0d. The estate workers employed for the walling were E. Walker, A. Larner and N. Paget.

Most of the monies required for the monument were raised by subscriptions and donations from Lord Sherborne and the farmers and cottagers.

A remembrance service, attended by the British Legion standard bearers from Northleach and the villagers, is held each year at the memorial.

The memorial is maintained by Mr L. Hayward on behalf of the Parish Council who are responsible for its upkeep.

CHAPTER SEVEN

The School

The school is an integral part of any village and when it is lost, there is a feeling that the heart is taken out of the community.

Sherborne is lucky in having retained its primary school, despite a threat of closure a few years ago. Albeit, about half of the pupils are transported in by a mini-bus, and in private cars driven by parents from neighbouring villages.

The earliest mention of a school in the village was a reference in Samuel Rudder's *New History of Gloucester 1651–2*, which reads:

> A ground called Cruickmore [which is allotted to the Sandyhill Farm] worth 40 shillings a year, is given towards the maintenance of a school master, Alexander Ready permitted the issues and profits of this ground to be applied to the use of a school so long as there was a master but I don't find that it was a permanent establishment.

However, the offer must have been taken up for a short while as a payment of £2 was received by the parish clerk around this time.

It is almost certain that Robert Raikes of Gloucestershire, along with the help of William Fox of the Manor, Clapton, was the founder of the early Sunday schools (one for girls and one for boys).

On 16 January 1791, an agreement was drawn up with reference to opening a Sunday school in the village, supported through voluntary subscription. The document reads:

> We whose names are subscribed, being thoroughly convinced of the great utility of Sunday Schools as a means of promoting true religion, and of rendering the lower class of the community more useful in their several stations, and better members of society, do with a view to promote so good an institution within this Parish, severally agree to pay into the hands of the Treasurer to be appointed for that purpose, the sums appearing against our respective names.

The subscriptions, ranging from 10s. 6d. to £5 5s. (a substantial amount in those days), were made by the following people: Lord and Lady Sherborne; three Miss Duttons; Mrs Dutton; Mr Walton; Mrs Manageot; Thos Stephens; Thos Fletcher; Robert Ecles; Henry Day; William Garne; Arthur Hale; Anthony Cooper; and Mr Hayward. The subscribers selected Mr Markham as treasurer, and Mr Stephens and Mr Ecles as visitors to the schools. An extract from the rules governing the

Sunday schools reads, 'That nothing whatever be taught in the schools but what is suited immediately to the design of the Sabbath and preserving young people from idleness, immorality and ignorance.'

Mr Cooper and Mr Hitchman were appointed as teachers of the boys school, and Mrs Ann St John of the girls school; all three were to receive an allowance of 1s. 6d. each per week.

The subscribers also directed that, every Sunday morning, the children should assemble in their respective school rooms precisely at 8 a.m. in the summer and 9 a.m. in the winter, with their hair combed, hands and faces washed, and dressed as decently as the circumstances of their parents would permit, that they constantly attend divine service (in the church) with their masters and mistresses, and that they return to their respective school rooms in two separate divisions, one for boys and one for girls, when they might be permitted to go home. But when divine service happened to be only once a day, the time of attending the schools had to be varied accordingly. They also directed that the children be instructed to read in the Old and New Testament and to learn their catechism, with a morning and evening prayer. It was agreed that these schools would commence as soon as proper books could be purchased.

An account, dated January 1792, reveals that all of the subscriptions were paid and that Mr Raikes was paid the sum of £5 'for books for use of the School'. Mrs St John and her daughter were paid for their services until 1 January 1800, and as there were no further payments recorded, presumably the village Sunday schools ended then.

The following information does not concern the village of Sherborne directly, but it does provide a great insight into the poverty which prevailed in years past. 'The Managers of the early Sunday Schools did not always content themselves with providing food solely for the mind. In some instances they were accustomed also to provide food and clothing for the body.' The village of Painswick, in which Mr Raikes took a deep interest, furnishes a good example in point. Mr Raikes records that on the day after Christmas Day in 1785, a bountiful dinner of beef, pudding and potatoes was given to the 350 children attending Painswick School. The donors of the feast themselves officiated as carvers and waiters. To illustrate how welcome this feast must have been, Mr Raikes adds:

When the meal was set before one boy it was observed that he did not eat. He was asked the reason, and the poor wretch said it was three days since he had had any food and his stomach was gone. However, by taking a little, his appetite at last returned. Another was asked if he had eaten so plentiful a meal this twelve months, 'No, nor these three last twelve months' replied the boy.

Church of England schools were established in 1824 by the 2nd Lord Sherborne, John Dutton, again with one school for boys and one for girls. Presumably these schools first operated in the vicinity of Sherborne House (probably in the rooms that had been used for Sunday school).

Sherborne school children photographed between 1868 and 1877.

A plaque, now believed to be in the hands of the National Trust, was recently discovered. On it was inscribed the words:

> If any of the parents of the children who come to my school are dissatisfied with the rules of it, I beg that those who are so, will take their children away instead of complaining to the School Mistress who has no power to change any of the rules I have laid down. If, after this notice, I find that complaints are still made I shall myself send away the children of the dissatisfied parents as those who come to the school must [?please] totally observe all the rules of it and no complaints must be made.

This was dated 20 September 1825, and signed M. Sherborne (Lady Mary Sherborne), who evidently regarded the girls school as her own.

When the village was rebuilt in 1830, one school was established where the village post office block now stands and the other on the site of the village social club. In *Kelly's Directory*, dated 1856, there is reference to Thomas Bagley being master and Mrs Phoebe Ann Hooper, mistress, in Lord Sherborne's schools.

In 1862, the two schools were combined under a master with one assistant. In *Kelly's Directory* of 1863, Edwin Terrel is named as master and Miss Ann Hooper, mistress.

The present school, opened in 1868, was built as a result of the generosity of the

3rd Lord Sherborne (James Dutton), at a cost of approximately £1,000. A bench mark on the school building states that it stands 436 feet above sea level.

In 1869 the school received an annual grant, and the average attendance was eighty-three. Children attending the school around this time had to pay, on Mondays, one penny per week, with farmers' children paying two pennies. Research has failed to determine when this payment ceased as the old school registers were sent to Gloucester several years ago and now cannot be traced.

An evening school, established in 1871, was attended by six pupils, the attendance rose to twenty-four by 1872.

The C. of E. school was inspected annually by HM Inspector of Schools and it is noted that the teaching staff, as well as the work of the scholars, came in for criticism. An extract from the inspector's report of 26 May 1874 states that 'the Pupil Teachers' paperwork on some subjects is unaccountably bad'. The children would have used slates and slate pencils to do their work at this time.

On 26 April 1875 the inspector reports that, 'The registers in use during the past year are partly insufficient and partly have been imperfectly kept. Total daily attendance must be entered at the foot of each page. A new Admission Book is desirable, which must be indexed and state the birthday of each child.'

The 1876 *Kelly's Directory* mentions that Mr and Mrs Henry Brew were school master and mistress. But by 1877 Mr V. Rose and his wife had taken these positions.

The inspector's report for 1881 reads, 'The school is in good order. The Infants and 2nd Standard are very well taught. Reading is very fair throughout the rest of the school, but much other work is only fair. Handwriting on examination papers is decidedly poor.'

In 1883 the inspector reported that, 'The lavatory is without water. It is too much for the teachers to carry the water needed by so many girls if they are to keep their needlework clean. This should be remedied.' (In this instance it is thought that the word 'lavatory' refers to wash room.)

Much attention was paid to needlework; the inspector's report of 1889 states that the hemming stitches in Standard I and II were very poor, and in Standard VI, 'When putting on a patch, attention should be paid to the warp and weft of the material. Singing is sweeter in some of the other villages in the Cotswolds.'

In 1891 the Inspector was pleased with the good work done, 'and the school had gone towards earning the Principal grant of fourteen shillings. Needlework had improved but there was room for improvement in parsing and mapping. The girls were behind the boys in Geography, a little more care in writing down Arithmetic was desirable and the meaning of recitation was not sufficiently understood.'

The following year, 1892, the inspector doubted whether the grant could be recommended, 'if the teacher under Article 68 is so largely withdrawn from the Infants for the instruction of the elder children'.

Mr V Rose started the headteacher's log book in 1896. The average attendance then was 82.9.

In June of that year, 'the causeway round the school buildings was asphalted to the great advantage of the scholars, especially the infants'. From 2 November to 7 December the school was closed owing to a measles epidemic.

1897   Jany.1st – Headteacher punished two boys for grossly assaulting two other lads following dismissal from school the previous day. Children were advised to bring handkerchiefs to school otherwise they would be punished.

Feby.5th – Punished several boys for following hounds instead of attending school [undoubtedly Ernest Margetts, aged 10, was among them as he could not resist running after the hounds].

April, 1897 – One of the biggest boys threw a stone at a horse in the street during playtime; the owner of the horse came into the playground and with the permission of the Headmaster gave the boy two stripes with his whip. The other boys were subsequently cautioned.

Miss C. Rose and Elsie Akerman had joined the staff as monitresses at this time.

The syllabus for 1898 was as follows. Recitation: Standard I, 'The Squirrel'; Standard II, 'A Night with a Wolf'; Standard III, 'The Mariners of England and Harvest Home'; Standard IV, 'Lay of the Last Minstrel'; Standards V, VI, VII, 'Fall of Wolsey'; and for VI and VII only, 'Young Lochinvar'. Songs for the Infants: 'Dolly at School', 'Eight White Sheep' and 'The Cunning Mouse'. General Knowledge: The Kitten, Songs for the older scholars: 'Oh the Sunny Summertime', 'Baby Roy', 'The Schoolboy's Foes', 'The Cuckoo' and 'The Lighthouse'.

In 1902 the County Council Education Committee was formed. In April 1903, Mr Turner from the surveyors department of the County Council called to make a thorough examination of both the exterior and interior of the school.

In the same year an indenture was drawn up between the Rt Hon. Lord Edward Sherborne and the vicar, Revd J. Willis, referring to the lease of the school and teacher's residence for a period of twenty-one years commencing 25 December 1902. The annual rent was set at 2s. 6d., payable on 25 December, the first payment due on 25 December 1903. The agreement was witnessed and signed by the two principals, plus the church wardens, George Freeman and Henry Mason of Windrush, and Robert Gray, Sherborne estate agent. On 12 February 1904, Miss Dutton visited the school and inspected needlework and composition exercises.

1904   May 6th – School was closed owing to a Scarlet Fever epidemic.

Octr. 14th – Physical exercises were first taught as directed by the Board of Education.

Novr. – Heavy snowfalls affected attendance.

1905   Feby.14th – Boys cautioned for smoking.

Lord Sherborne gave prizes for good attendance, arithmetic and needlework.

June – New desks arrived from Glasgow, and girls took cookery lessons on Friday afternoons.

June 23rd – A Swallow's nest was discovered on the School premises [to this day swallows still build their nests in the school front porch].

1906   The school was enlarged in order to take in more pupils [this must have been the time the infant room was added].

Sept.21st – Seven of the Upper Standard girls were entered for a course of lectures on dairying. Lectures to be given, on Thursday and Friday mornings after Registers, by Miss Priday a County Council lecturer. The course ended on October 16th.

Novr.16th – Boys had instruction of three lectures on Farriery, four boys received prizes for their essays, on the 'The Structure of the Horses Foot', from the Chairman of the Governors, George Freeman of Stones Farm.

1907   March 15th – Children were allowed a half day holiday in order to witness the funeral of Lady Sherborne. Mr Terrel, the Headmaster 35 years earlier, visited the school.

There were frequent entries of children being admitted under the age of five, some as young as three years old.

One of the older boys was caned for swearing in the playground, and one of the girls for severely kicking another. The boys were warned against 'interfering' with the girls on their way home from school.

March 22nd – A parcel of seeds etc. received, for use after Easter, in connection with the new special subject of 'School Gardening'.

April 12th – Thirteen of the older boys began school gardening under the instruction of Mr Mitchell, Head Gardener to Lord Sherborne.

April 26th – Mr Hollingsworth, County Council Inspector in Horticulture, inspected the gardens declaring them to be a splendid success.

1908   When the Inspector visited this year he suggested that the high curtain [used since the school's inception to separate the classes] be replaced by a low wooden screen, also that guards should be provided for the stoves in both rooms. The latter was a requirement of the Board of Education and should be carried out with the least possible delay.

May 25th – Empire Day was celebrated by children assembling round the Union Jack in the boys' playground and singing patriotic songs interspersed with cheering. Lessons regarding the Empire and its Flag were given during the day, but there was no holiday. [When Empire Day was celebrated in the following and subsequent years, a half-day holiday was granted in honour of the occasion.] Six new desks arrived from Glasgow.

July 9th – Two boys caned for persistent trespass on the Teacher's garden path, children were allowed to have newspapers for silent reading.

Novr. 16th – 1st Medical Inspection, by Dr Blake and Nurse Trueman, of all children in the school.

1909.   March 1st – The Inspector reported that too much work on the '3 R's' was done in the afternoon, some of the lessons on the Time Table should be interchanged to obviate this. He also suggested a glazed folding partition instead of the present curtain would be of great service in allowing the work to be carried on more quietly. 'Curtains' do not exclude sound and are objectionable on sanitary grounds [HMI Mr de Sausmarez].

Schoolboy gardeners, *c*.1923. Back row, left to right: L. Pratley, G. Tyres, W. Petrie. Middle row: S. Wilsdon, F. Margetts, G. Smith, F. Lester. Front row: L. Cyphus, P. Higgins, A. Larner, A. Margetts.

THE SHERBORNE TROOP OF BOY SCOUTS.

Sherborne troop of boy scouts was started by G.A. Knowlson B.A. (Headteacher) in April 1910.

1910   March 18th – Mr Rose and his daughter left the School with goodbyes exchanged [Mr Rose had been headteacher for thirty-three years].

April 18th – The School re-opened after the school holidays with a new staff; Mr G.A. Knowlson B.A., Headteacher, Miss Bennett, Assistant Mistress and Miss Leach, Infant Teacher. A new requisition was made for painting and stationery materials. Mr Knowlson reported that discipline in the school was lax and work very backward, behaviour was generally very good. The number of pupils on the register was 94 (soon increased to 97). Cleanliness of every scholar was a source of gratification.

April 15th – (Behaviour soon lapsed) Four boys were soundly punished for acting in a disrespectful manner to the Assistant Mistress. Mr Knowlson became the Hon. Secretary of the Boy Scouts and several elder boys were induced to join the village Patrol.

May 13th – The older boys subscribed towards the purchase of a football, and the sum of two shillings and one penny was collected.

July 16th – The School Cricket Team played its 1st match against Aldsworth School and won by an innings and 70 runs.

Oct. – There was considerable absence among the girls for baby minding at home. A School Cleaner was appointed.

Sept. 30th – Measurements were taken for the new glazed partition screen.

Novr. 25th – Notice was received from the North of England School Furnishing Co. that a CLIMAX partition screen was on rail and would be put in the school during the weekend. The screen did not arrive but the man engaged to erect it did!

Decr. 2nd – A holiday was given on Monday so that the new glazed partition could be erected in the main room [That same screen is still in use in the main schoolroom today. During the author's schooldays, the noise from each classroom still penetrated through to the other, which at times was very disturbing. It is difficult to comprehend what the situation must have been like with only a curtain dividing the rooms].

1910   August – Children submitted entries to the local Flower Show and won prizes for painting, writing, arithmetic, needlework, essays, garden plots and collections of vegetables. Prize cards were exhibited on the School wall.

1911   January – Children complained of the cold, the outside temperature was 35°F, wood had to be used in the stove as the fuel ordered the previous week had not arrived.

Apart from the annual inspection from HM Inspectors, regular Diocesan inspections were made. After one such occurrence, in which a complaint was raised, the Headmaster received the following letter:

'April 28th, – Dear Mr Knowlson, Mr Willis [Vicar of Sherborne for many years] showed me your letter referring to my report on your

School, when I went to Windrush yesterday. I recollect the circumstances perfectly, and the mistake is mine entirely. I ought not to have mentioned the written work of Standard I at all, as it was only given to keep them quiet. The fact is, the circumstances slipped my memory when I was going through my paperwork. Please explain to the teacher that I have amended the Report as follows, "The written work as a whole is good." Yours truly A.W. Douglas of the Rectory, Hatherop, Glos.'

December – The Headmaster purchased 40 books for a School Library with money he obtained from the Coronation Festivities Committee.

1912   Jany.7th to March 29th – School closed for measles epidemic.

August – During the summer holidays a new heating apparatus, of the low pressure furnace type, was installed taking the place of the slow combustion stoves. [This is presumably when the radiators were installed. No record was made of the stoker, but Mr William (Bill) Stevens carried out the task for many years, followed by his son Frank. Upon Frank's death, Ron Hicks, his brother-in-law, took over until the furnace was replaced by an electrically controlled heater. Extra radiators were installed in the classrooms and controlled from inside the school.]

Sept. – There was an epidemic of Scarlet Fever, ten cases were reported to the fever hospital [tin-roofed buildings] at Farmington.

1913   March – New piano arrives at the school.

May – The Scarlet Fever epidemic lasted until this month, only to be followed by measles, resulting in the death of one child. There were also cases of ringworm, chicken pox and one tuberculosis case.

Decr. – Mr Knowlson left the school.

1914   January to May 26th – Mr Welch succeeded as Headteacher.

June 15th – Mr H Demer was appointed Headteacher with Mrs Demer, Assistant, Miss Whitehead, Infant Teacher and Georgina Saunders as Monitress. While Mrs Demer took a two week course in Cookery, her place was taken by Miss A.V. Tunrer, a supply teacher. Mr Demer's salary was £110 per annum. There were 85 children on the register. Mr Demer reported that he found the school and the materials in a very dirty condition. Handwork tools were spoiled through being allowed to get in a terribly rusty condition. Arithmetic appears to be the weakest subject throughout the school, mental work being especially very weak. Discipline very lax, too much talking and wandering round the schoolroom both in and out of school hours. Silent reading is a farce not 10% of them knowing anything of the matter.

Novr. 19th – First lesson of woodwork was given for boys over the age of 11 [Mr Demer was an excellent carpenter].

1915   June 15th – Mr Demer left the school for Military Service and joined

Sherborne school football team, 1921–22. Back row, left to right: Charlie Stevens, Francis Lester, Eric Demer, Mr Demer (Headmaster). Centre row: Luther Pratley, Tom Saunders, –?–. Front row: Albie Larner, Steve Williams, Leslie Turner, Stuart Saunders, Fred Margetts.

the Royal Gloucester Artillery. Mrs Demer was left in charge of the school during his absence.

June 21st – Outbreak of Diphtheria – school was closed for one week. [Outbreaks and absences lasted until the beginning of the Autumn term in September.]

1917   Novr. – Mr Demer returned to school to take up his duties.

1920   June 23rd – A box of library books was dispatched from Gloucester to Bourton-on-the-Water railway station [this, evidently, was the beginning of the library book service].

Novr. 12th – A collection was made in the school for Dr Barnado's, resulting in a total sum of £3 17s. 10½d. [collections for Dr Barnado's are still made in the school].

1922   Feby. – Mrs Isobel Petrie was paid 16s. 8d. per month as school cleaner and William Stevens 14s. per month for stoking the furnace.

1927   Jany. 19th – Ron Walker was the first Sherborne pupil to attend the re-established 'Westwoods Grammar School' at Northleach.

September – Reg. Clarke followed Ron Walker to 'Westwoods'. [Later in life he became Bishop of Rhodesia.]

1930   Sept. – Sybil Margetts was the first Sherborne girl to attend the Northleach Grammar School. She was accompanied by John Houlton who was joining his brother Geoff. [Tragically, John failed to return from the Far East after the Second World War. His name, along with that of George Dixon, was added to those already inscribed on the war memorial.]

1934   Novr. 1st – Free milk commenced in the schools in Gloucestershire. Sixty-eight children took advantage of the scheme at Sherborne. The milk was supplied by William Tremaine.

Novr. 23rd – Two boys, Lionel Hockey and Edward Thornton, collided whilst playing football. Edward was knocked against the very low wall surrounding the school and fell into the road. Mr Demer rendered first aid and took the boy to Bourton Hospital, where he was detained.

Decr. 3rd – As Mr Demer left Bourton Hospital with Thornton, the Matron handed him an account of the charges; 10s. for x-ray and 10s. for part cost of his stay in hospital. This account was passed to Revd George Warner, the Vicar, for payment. As a direct result of this accident, the official School Correspondent promised to have an efficient guard erected along the playground wall. [This was later supplemented with the addition of the hedge which is still in existence.]

1935   May 6th and 7th – School closed for Silver Jubilee celebrations of the reign of HM King George V and Queen Mary. An oak tree was

Sherborne junior school children, c. 1929. Back row, left to right: Rose Lockey, Doris Turner, Sybil Margetts, Phyllis Wilsdon, Ernest Large, John Houlton, George Johnson, John Newport. Second row: Harry Taylor, Leslie Palmer, Edward Hunt, Cyril Large, Cyril Scotford, Albert Ash, Laurie Hooper, Edward Bullock. Third row: Peggy Taylor, Myrtle Larner, Violet Mills, Nellie Saunders, Marjorie Tye, Barbara Bullock, Joan Turner, Tina Margetts. Front row: Lionel Morse, Sydney Petrie, Kenneth Panter, William Hooper, George Dixon.

planted at the bottom of the playground, by the war memorial, to commemorate this happy occasion.

1942   May 27th – Children were allowed to assist with potato planting on the farms.

Octr. 9th – School closed for potato harvest.

Novr. 9th – School lunches commenced in the Reading Room, Mrs D. Mosson was appointed cook. Forty-nine children and three teachers had a cooked mid-day meal, the Revd G. Warner and Mr T. Matthews, a school manager and JP, also attended as guests. The pupils paid 5s. a week for their meals.

1944   July 10th – Miss Myrtle Larner joined the staff as Infant Teacher and Mrs Emma Stevens was employed as Canteen Assistant.

1946   August – Tragically, Mr Demer died whilst on holiday following a sudden illness, after 32 years service to the school and village.

Mrs Margaret Mate, an octogenarian now residing in Norfolk, recalls that, 'Mr Demer was a strict disciplinarian, who would use the cane even on girls if he felt they deserved it'. Mr Demer was very much respected by the village community, especially so by his former pupils who were indebted to him for their solid educational grounding, even if some of them did suffer as a result of his wrath during their schooldays.

He was much involved with all aspects of village life, with the football and cricket teams on the sporting side, and with social activities such as the annual village fête, whist drives and dances.

There is a plaque, erected on a wall in the school which reads: 'In memory of Harry Horace Demer, for 32 years Headmaster of Sherborne School 1914–1946. This tablet is erected as a mark of esteem by past and present scholars.'

1946   Sept. – Mr. Phillips was installed as a supply teacher until the end of the Autumn term.

1947   Jany. 6th – Mr J.K.P. Herrin took up his duties as Headteacher and found within a very short time attendances were severely curtailed by the extreme weather of that winter. By this time children were brought in by bus from Clapton following the closure of their village school.

Jany. 29th – Snow prevented the bus from running, the school was closed for two days but re-opened for those children within walking distance. The attendance varied between eleven and twenty.

Feby. 20th – Bus reached Clapton after an absence of three weeks.

March 3rd – The school fuel supply ran out; two days later the worst blizzard in living memory struck, completely isolating the village. The snow was 18–36 inches deep all around the school and no children attended.

March 10th – Several of the roads were opened to single lane traffic.

March 12th – The fuel supply was restored and school resumed.

March 17th – After another heavy snowfall, rain followed which, combined with the thaw, caused flooding. With the additional

Villagers gathered in the school on Coronation Day 1953.

problem of fallen trees, the school bus, once again, failed to get through.

March 21st – The ground around the school was at last clear of snow and ice for the first time in eight weeks.

1948   July 19th – Miss Browning, and eighteen pupils from Aldsworth school, joined Mr Herrin and Miss Larner and eighteen Sherborne pupils on a day visit to Birmingham. They departed Sherborne, by coach, at 7.45 a.m. The itinerary included; a tour through the suburbs, a visit to Hodgekiss Ltd – manufacturers of high class jewellery, lunch at Loxton St. Secondary Modern, a visit to Aston Villa Football Club, a tour of the industrial area and BSA factory, tea at The British Restaurant in Shirley and finally returning to Sherborne at 9 p.m.

In return, the boys from Loxton School were invited to a week's camp at Sherborne to learn map reading. By kind permission of Mr Mosey [principal of King's School for Boys] they all visited Sherborne House, former home to Lord and Lady Sherborne. The itinerary also included; a visit to Chedworth Villa, Northleach Church, Lodge Park, Sherborne Farm to see the up-to-date milking methods and Home Farm to see modern farm machinery and poultry keeping.

The weekend was given to walks, sketching and games. In the cricket match Sherborne defeated Loxton by 63 runs to 25. Meals were taken in the canteen where staff were supplemented by members of the Women's Institute.

The Loxton boys returned home bronzed, happy and looking forward to their visit to Liverpool Docks. Sherborne children were to visit Bristol and Avon Docks as part of a new course of study on the export and import trade of Great Britain.

Sept. 30th – Elsie Larner and Emma Stevens ended their duties as Canteen Cook and Assistant, respectively, after five years' service.

Octr. 1st – New canteen staff appointed were; Mrs Dorothy Stevens, cook and Mrs Gwen Cambray, assistant.

1950   Jany. 1st – Mrs Sybil Meadwell [later to become Mrs Longhurst] commenced duty as a part-time school Clerk, to cope with the increasing amount of clerical work involved in the running of the school.

1951   July – Mrs Demer retired from her post as Assistant Mistress, having taught for 37 years.

1953   June – A flagpole was erected at the bottom of the playground, by the War Memorial, in recognition of the Coronation of Queen Elizabeth II who succeeded to the throne the previous year. The school was closed for the celebrations which were marred by the continuous heavy rainfall.

1954   Myrtle Larner left her employment as Infant's Teacher.

1959   Decr. – Mrs Joyce Hall was engaged as assistant teacher.

1961   Octr. – Mrs Margaret Shepherd commenced the post as school cleaner following the departure of Mrs E. Robinson. By this time pupils over the age of eleven were attending either the Secondary Modern at Bourton-on-the-Water or Westwoods Grammar at Northleach.

1965   It was about this time that Little Rissington C. of E. school was closed, with the intention that the pupils should be transferred to Bourton Council School, but as that school was within the 3-mile boundary, transport would not be provided. The Revd H. Cheales, of Wyck Rissington, did a little research into the options open to the affected parents. He discovered that the pupils could be transferred to another C. of E. school in the area if it suited. The children were transferred to Upper Slaughter school, where, however, the increase in numbers caused some considerable inconvenience. After much consultation, and with Mr Herrin's approval, it transpired that approximately eighteen, somewhat bewildered, pupils ended up at Sherborne with transport provided. The new pupils soon settled down to their new surroundings.

1966/67 A new 'Terrapin' buildings was erected for use by the Infant class,

Sherborne junior and senior school children, c. 1958. Back row, left to right: Bronwyn Beckford, Ann Harris, June Partlow, Valerie Lester, Hazel Stevens, Wendy Sallis, Jennifer Hicks, –?–, Michael Wood. Centre row: Susan Beckford, Jennifer Henvest, –?–, Kathleen Shepherd, Mr J. Herrin (Headmaster), Pamela Johnson, Sylvia Jarman, Jennifer Wilsdon, Wendy World. Front row: Johnny Young, David Hayward, William Johnson, Colin Vincent, Annette Hanks, Jane Hooper, John Longhurst, Robert Preston, Grahame Saunders, Bill Limbrick.

their old room was altered to accommodate a kitchen, larder and store room.

1968   Sept. 15th – An important day in the school's history. One hundred years on from the foundation of the present building.

Sept. 18th – On a lovely, warm and sunny day, staff, pupils and governors of the school, together with parents and guests gathered to celebrate the centenary of the school. The Revd Westmorland, parish vicar, opened proceedings. The distinguished guests were; the Rt Hon. George Dutton (for his brother Lord Sherborne), The Rt Revd Forbes Horan, Bishop of Tewkesbury and Chairman of the Diocesan Council of Education, Col. Jenkins, Chairman of the County Education Committee and Mr W.E. Gardner, the Assistant Education Officer. The Bishop of Tewkesbury presented to each pupil an inscribed prayer book donated by the Parochial Church Council. The Rt Hon. George Dutton planted a magnolia tree, in the school playground, to mark the event. Light refreshments were served to all.

1971   March 31st – Mr Herrin retired from his post as headmaster, after 24 years of dedicated work, and was sadly missed. He had taken a keen interest in the social and sporting activities in the village, especially in the football and cricket teams. The WI were very much indebted to him for his invaluable assistance in helping them to overcome many difficulties encountered during their early foundation years.

Reference ought to be made here to the considerable number of pupils who, during Mr Herrin's time as headmaster, left the school to continue their studies at Westwoods Grammar and Bourton Comprehensive, and on to further education at training schools and universities.

April – Mr Sims was appointed temporary headmaster until December.

1972   January – Mr D. Thompson took up his duties as headmaster. Mrs Vera Hayward joined the staff as lunchtime supervisor on the departure of Mrs Mills, who had carried out the duty for many years. This year also heralded the foundation of The International Academy for Continuous Education in Sherborne House, by Mr John Bennett, Principal. Students from all over the world attended the Academy, many bringing their families with them. The children of the students at the Academy swelled the numbers attending the village school and brought with them some unusual problems. One child, a Japanese boy named Tetsuya Denda (Teddy), could not speak a word of English. With some assistance from the Education Authority and the dedication and patience of his teachers, it was not long before Teddy had completely mastered the language, and his written work had surpassed that of many of the local children. Teddy was also an excellent violinist.

Some of the other children remembered were Jason Connery, whose mother Diane Cilento had been married to the actor Sean Connery, the Linguards, from Norway, a very musical family, and Ibrahim from Turkey.

Mr Thompson revived Morris Dancing, with Mr Linguard providing the music. A team of boys performed at the school fête in the grounds of Sherborne House. At Christmas Mr Thompson, with the help of Mr Linguard, took a group of children around the village to perform and sing Christmas carols. When he left, Mr Linguard took the idea of morris dancing back to his native Norway.

Mr Thompson recalls that he failed to recognize Jason Connery's acting ability, in not picking him for the lead role in the school Christmas play, Jason is, of course, now well-known as an actor.

It was during Mr Thompson's term of office that the Gloucestershire Education Committee proposed closing either Aldsworth, Great Barrington or Sherborne school. This unpopular proposition resulted in a considerable amount of correspondence, meetings and bitter feelings in the local community.

1977   June – The school was closed in celebration of the Silver Jubilee of the reign of Queen Elizabeth II.

1979   April – Mr Thompson left the school to take up the post of headmaster at Andoversford School.

Mr Williams, from Northleach, was appointed temporary headmaster for one term.

July – Mr N. Turner became headmaster.

The school fête continued annually, with the displays of country dancing given by the children proving to be a very popular event.

Our resident actor, Eric Dodson, succeeded in procuring the services of two well-known personalities to open the fête on separate occasions, namely Kathy Staff (Nora Batty) and Lynette McMorrough (Glenda from *Crossroads*).

Mr Turner closed the fêtes with barn dances, held in the evenings in a barn on Stones Farm, by kind permission of Mr Peter Summers.

Another interest was the formation of a gymnastics club. The children would, again, perform annually at the fête.

A six-a-side soccer team was founded. A competition, to decide the name, was held among the pupils. Mark Hamilton, of Little Rissington, won with his entry 'Trojans'.

Mr Turner created a school shield based on the Sherborne coat of arms which he copied, from the crest displayed on the gates at Cheltenham Lodges, while sitting in his car one very wet Saturday. It was during this time that the Education Authority finally decided to close both Aldsworth and Great Barrington schools. The pupils from Aldsworth were transferred to Bibury and the Great Barrington pupils to Sherborne School. However, with so much ill feeling created by the situation, some of the Great Barrington students went to Burford.

The old telephone exchange, on becoming redundant, was taken over by the Sherborne estate. It was suggested that the building might be rented by the Education Committee for the use by the school. Several plans and suggestions for its use were tendered; one being to turn it into a pottery shed, but a spare kiln was unavailable at the time and the idea was eventually overruled on the grounds of safety.

The Education Committee finally decided that the building would be too much of a liability. For a short while the children used it to house small pets such as rabbits and guinea pigs.

Eventually the building was acquired for use as a play school. Myrtle Larner had started a play school, in September 1968, at the home of Mr and Mrs W Tremaine. The location of the school had changed several times over the years and, just at that time, they had to vacate the premises in the stable block because it was advertised for sale. A number of modifications were required before the building complied with the health and safety regulations necessary to the proper running of a toddlers play school. Happily, the play school is still in use today, run successfully by Myrtle and her daughter, Hilary.

One hair-raising occurrence which happened during the tenure of Mr Turner, was the night the old summer house on the school lawn caught fire, ignited by the heat from a compost heap sited too close to the building. Mr and Mrs Turner, who were still in their night attire, were assisted in quelling the blaze by close neighbours, Harry and Mavis Taylor.

Unfortunately the old summer house was razed to the ground.

Immediately prior to Mr Turner relinquishing his post as headmaster, his second child Oliver was born.

1983   Decr. – Mr Turner moved to Norfolk upon his appointment as headteacher of a primary school in Newton Flotnam.

1984   Jany. – Mr Buck, a Gloucestershire supply headteacher, was engaged for one term.

April – Mr R. Rodgers was confirmed as headmaster.

July – Sybil Longhurst retired from her post (which had been upgraded to school secretary due to the ever increasing quantity of paperwork) after 34 years service. She was succeeded by Mrs Ann Porter from Chedworth.

Mr Rodgers has taken the children on visits to the weaving mill at Filkins and the Gloucester Docks. He has also taken the juniors on an adventure holiday.

1986   The juniors worked on a project in commemoration of the 900 years since the publication of the Domesday Book. They studied the survey of the land and its uses, the farms and their acreages, and past life of the villagers. All this was stored on a computer disc and sent to Gloucester for storage in the archives.

1989   Novr. 26th – The National Trust invited the school children to assist in planting a number of beech trees along the walk, recently opened, through the Sherborne Park grounds. All of the trees were labelled with the names, in pairs, of the children taking part as follows:

Carl and Sally-Ann Abraham
Nicholas and Thomas Pepper
James Bennett and Paul Cook
Michael and Jenny Louks
Phillip Colmer and Kirk Wood
Becky and Laura Smith
Tim and Stephen Robinson
Rachael Limbrick and Beverly Strange
Katy and Emlyn Long
Jason Squires and Rhian Hadley
Alexia Tidmarsh and Kelly Swallow
Hannah Cooper and Ann Souter
Russel Griffin and Byron Hadley
John Westacott and Arty Palmer
Karl Hayward and Johnathon Parker
James and Vicky Wilkes
Hannah Collins and Katie Louks
Alice Waltham and Rosie Barton (National Trust helper)

The present school staff comprises:

headmaster, Mr R. Rodgers
infant's teacher, Mrs J. Hall
part-time teacher, Mrs Kelsey
secretary, Mrs A. Porter
cook, Mrs M. Bunting
lunchtime supervisor, Mrs V. Hayward
cleaner, Mrs M. Shepherd.

CHAPTER EIGHT

Victorian and Edwardian Memories

The living standards of the past, which fortunately have improved beyond belief since the beginning of the twentieth century, appear quite alien to the present, young generation.

In constructing the recent social history of Sherborne, we have been most fortunate in obtaining many childhood reminiscences from several village octogenarians which, together with memories and stories recalled by parents and grandparents, have provided us with a wealth of material.

Poverty was very widespread, among the working classes, due to low wages, poor living standards and large families, which quite often included an elderly grandparent living in the same house. There would be no financial help from the grandparent, as the retirement pension was not introduced in Britain until 1909, and even then just a few shillings were paid to men only, on reaching the age of seventy. It was not until 1925 that contributary pensions were introduced. These were extended in 1929, whereby persons insured under the health insurance scheme paid an extra sum weekly, ensuring that both husband and wife each received a pension of 10s. per week on reaching the age of sixty-five. In the event of the death of the husband, the weekly pension was granted to his widow with a small allowance for each child.

When children reached the age of twelve they were allowed to leave school if they had a job awaiting them, but in order to do this they had to obtain a labour certificate from the head teacher. Names had to be submitted for this a few days before the end of term, thereby allowing time for the certificate to be prepared. One villager, by the name of Joseph Margetts, applied for and received such a certificate from Mr Rose (the head teacher at that time) when his second son Henry John left school (see opposite).

The few extra shillings earned by a child, would be of some assistance, but at what price? Young boys were expected to be out in all winds and weathers, only to be paid a pittance for long hours and hard work.

Domestic chores were very laborious and time-consuming. There was no gas or electricity available, not even a piped water supply, so every drop of water required, whether for washing of hands and face, pot washing, or for washing the floor, had to be heated. If a bracket was not used, the saucepans or kettle when placed on the burning wood or coals, could often slip resulting in the water spilling

The School.
Sherborne.
Apr. 5/92.

Mr Margetts,
I enclose a certificate for Harry.
I was very sorry to lose him as he did all his work, & especially his drawing, very carefully & well.
Thanking you for sending him so regularly & hoping you were satisfied with his progress at school
I remain
Yrs truly
E. Rose.

Headmaster's letter which accompanied Harry Margett's labour certificate in 1892.

into the fire and sending out a cloud of ashes and an accompanying foul smell into the air.

Some elderly villagers were still using a large black pot to do their cooking as late as the 1930s, especially on Sundays when the dinner (as the normal mid-day meal was called), which consisted of a meat pudding cooked in a basin, prelined and topped with a suet crust, covered with a floured cloth tied around the top of the basin with fine white string, was placed in the pot of boiling water. Several kinds of vegetables (whatever was in season) would be cooked in specially made white-string nets, added to the pot.

Overall, the living was very plain, but wholesome. As meat was generally unavailable to the average family, rabbit proved a common dish (except in the breeding season), either baked whole or jointed, and made into tasty stews and pies. Rabbits were often poached from the many small woods surrounding the village, providing the whereabouts of the gamekeeper was known. Often the gamekeeper turned a blind eye to this pastime, favourite among the young lads of the village, providing the game birds were not disturbed and no damage was done to the walls and fences. In addition, a few coppers could be obtained for the skins from the rag and bone man who regularly travelled through the villages.

Villagers leaving church on Club Day in the early 1900s.

Pigeons were also plentiful and for just a few pence made a tasty meal, either stewed with suet dumplings and root vegetables, or made into a pie.

A roast chicken or a joint of meat with Yorkshire pudding was a positive luxury for the average working family. On the rare occasion it appeared on the menu, the meat was cooked on a trivet in the roasting tin and, as it reached the final stages of cooking, the batter pudding was added so that the juices from the meat would give the pudding a distinctive flavour. The dripping, drained from the tin before the pudding was added, was allowed to cool and when spread on bread or toast proved a real favourite for breakfast. A pound of dripping could always be purchased from the cook at Sherborne House for the princely sum of 3d. There were no worries then about the consumption of excess fat causing heart or weight problems, in fact it was positively encouraged to keep the body warm and the common cold at bay.

Pieces of home-cured ham or bacon or, alternatively, roly-poly bacon pudding were a frequent feature on the midday table. Most householders would fatten a pig which, when killed, would keep hunger at bay for many a meal. Joints of pig meat (for it was never referred to as pork) were really delicious and, due mainly to the fact that the carcass was burnt in straw to remove the hairs instead of being porked in boiling water, had a taste to be remembered. Before deep freezes were invented, the storage of meat was not a simple task, so friends and relatives were often 'given' a joint on the understanding that this generosity would be repaid when their own animal was slaughtered.

After having been salted and preserved, sides of bacon, comprising more fat than lean, could frequently be seen hanging on kitchen walls. Hams, hocks and chines (the backbone, jointed) were also prepared in this fashion. The liver and tenderloins made tasty fries, the heart was stuffed and baked, and the well-cleaned and boiled chitterlings were consumed with relish. Delicious faggots were made from the lights which were boiled, seasoned and breadcrumbed, and then wrapped in pieces of gossamer veil peeled from the leaf of fat. Lard, some scented with sprigs of rosemary leaves to use as a spread on bread or toast, and the remainder left unflavoured and used for cooking, was another by-product of the leaf of fat. The small pieces of fat remaining after the melting process were called 'scratchings' and were eaten on slices of toast.

The dried pigs bladder was inflated and enjoyed as a football by the village boys or tied to a stick for the 'fool' in morris dancing and the mummers plays. In fact, Charlie Jones was heard to say that the only part of the pig that wasn't used was its squeal!

Pig feed comprised of a mash of boiled kitchen scraps and vegetable peelings added to a meal known as 'sharpes'. During the potato harvest the mash could be supplemented by the addition of small potatoes, however, many of these little 'taters' found their way back to the cottage where, after being cooked in their skins, they were peeled, sprinkled with salt and eaten with cheese or slices of bread and butter, or consumed on their own.

> 'My dear beloved brethren,
> Isn't it a sin,
> When you peel potatoes

To throw away the skin.
The skin feeds the pig
And the pig feeds you,
My dear beloved brethren,
Isn't that true?'

For those who worked with the sheep the advent of spring provided another delicacy, baked lambtail pie (in those days the lambs' tails were docked after a few weeks, whereas nowadays they are ringed at birth to prevent growth). They were first immersed in boiling water then dried, singed to remove any remaining hair and finally rinsed in salt water. The tails, were then alternated with layers of sliced, hard-boiled egg in a pie dish with a little seasoning and stock, and then the contents covered by a pastry topping.

When little or no meat was available, a filling mid-day meal consisted of jam roly poly or a plain suet pudding, sliced and sprinkled with sugar or spread with treacle (the addition of a few currants before cooking resulted in the ever-popular spotted dick). Other alternatives were boiled apple pudding or the good, old-fashioned rice pudding.

Whatever manner of meal was cooked, regardless of the means of cooking it, the dirty dishes had to be washed. This was accomplished in a bowl on the kitchen table, by adding either washing soda or soap flakes to the water that had been boiled in the kettle over the fire. Thus, coping with pots thick with grease and soot from the fire was not an easy task. Once washed, the dishes were upturned on to a tray to drain. Very few cottages would have had the luxury of a kitchen sink!

Up to the 1930s, candles or paraffin lamps provided lighting and this was another source of toil as they required daily attention; wicks needed trimming, the paraffin had to be replenished, glasses and globes (if used) had to be cleaned of smoke from the previous night – a very unpleasant but necessary task if maximum light was to be obtained. The flame, blown by the ever-present draughts, would project strange shadows on the walls (not for the faint-hearted), and tallow would drip down the sides of the candle used to light one to bed. The families who laboured on the farm or the estate, had the use of hurricane lamps – a wonderful invention.

In the early years of this century coal was expensive at 1s. per hundredweight, and few families could afford to buy even half that amount. Thus, the main source of fuel was wood, fallen from the huge trees growing in the surrounding countryside and gathered from the fields by the family. Large amounts of wood were used to get the fire going as quickly as possible in order to boil the kettle for the early morning 'cuppa'.

During the 1930s timber merchants, by the name of Brown Brothers, assisted by the Charlton Brothers, brought a team of men down from Yorkshire to fell a number of the large trees selected, by the estate, to be thinned from the woods. The men were lodged either with various families around the village or in mobile caravans (one of these, a green four-wheeled caravan, was still to be found until a few years ago, on Haycroft Farm, in a wood called The Grove). The accompanying teams of horses were stabled at Home Farm.

The tree felling was accomplished with manual labour, using sharp axes or large,

The Brown brothers' team of horses hauling tree trunks to be loaded on to steam wagons in the early 1930s.

two-man, cross-cut saws. Teddy Margetts, who worked for his uncle Clem Jones, the local haulier engaged by the estate to clear away the limbs and brashwood, recalled that one of the team of woodmen, nicknamed 'Soaker' (owing to his fondness for a few pints of ale), was an excellent axeman; he could fell a tree in half the time taken by two other men, and could judge to within a few inches exactly where the tree would fall.

Sold to the villagers for a few shillings each, the tops of the fallen trees, comprising the smaller branches and brashwood, could provide a cottage with fuel for many months. It was quite a familiar sight to see a whole family setting off, with a truck or an old perambulator loaded with saws and axes, to start work cutting the wood into manageable lengths and tying the brashwood into bundles for pea sticks or kindling.

Mrs Saysome was seen daily carrying wood home, slung across her shoulder, the amount she could carry equal to that of any man. 'You wouldn't see wood like this lying around if Mrs Saysome was alive today', is a remark often made by those who can remember her, when coming across wood lying in the fields.

The trimmed tree trunks were loaded on to the timber carriages by using a system of pulleys and a team of horses. The loaded carriages were then pulled across the uneven fields to a suitable site, where they were attached to Foden steam wagons and taken approximately five miles to Bourton-on-the-Water railway station for onward transmission to the timber mill. Mick Driver, of Bourton-on-the-Water, who was but a slip of a lad at the time, remembered the excitement

West Lodges. Mrs Morris and her daughters outside the cottage the National Trust now hope to make into a Museum. The cottage on the right of the pair is now the home of the National Trust warden.

experienced by him and his pals while keeping watch for the steam wagons approaching the station; the sparks from the engines lit up the darkening skies like fireworks. The fascination of those timber wagons remained with Mick throughout his life, as he grew up to work in the timber trade.

Peter, son of Dennis Brown of the original Brown Brothers, was a pupil at King's School while it was in Sherborne. The Brown family timber business, run by Peter Brown, still exists in Gloucestershire to this day.

Whiling away the long winter evenings, up until the late 1920s when radio came on the scene, taxed even the most fertile imagination. Family card games, snakes and ladders, draughts and shove ha'penny helped to pass away the hours. Rings and dart matches were played on the boards commonly found hanging on the back of the kitchen door. Reading was not common as books were relatively rare in the homes of the average working family.

The advent of the radio brought irreversible change. When it first appeared many squabbles were fought over the headphones that had to be worn in order to listen to the programmes. The passage of time saw inevitable improvements, one of which was the built-in loudspeaker; Mr Handy, farmer at Haycroft, was the first person in the village to have such a set. Mr Demer, the village school headmaster at that time, made a set and allowed the children back into school to listen to *Children's Hour* in the days of the 'Uncle Mac' programmes.

Batteries to operate the radio sets, required weekly recharging even if used only moderately. The recharging service was provided at a cost of 6d. by either Fred

Taylor, the estate electrician, or by the man in charge of the 'shop on wheels', who would collect the batteries one week and return them the next. Thus having two such batteries was imperative. The shop travelled through the villages each week selling household and gardening items, paraffin and mats etc. Television was a thing of the future.

A worthwhile hobby, practised in many homes, was the making of rag rugs. These rugs, as the name indicates, were made out of strips of woollen cloth (approximately 3 inches by 1 inch), cut from discarded clothes and pegged into an opened and washed flour or sugar sack, then backed by a similar material once the pegging was completed.

Most cottage floors consisted of quarry tiles or flagstones covered by linoleum or, most commonly, cocount matting. Every week, before the floor could be swept and scrubbed, the matting had to be taken up and well shaken. They provided a haven for the dust and dirt carried in from the roads and pavements, which consisted of crushed and rolled stone, easily picked up by hobnailed boots, unlike the tarmacadam roads that were to come later. The mats, when shaken or beaten, produced clouds of dust which filled the air. With a daily trampling by heavy boots and a constant patter of bare feet, the matting soon wore into holes and so the rag rugs were put to good service.

The stone floors had to be scrubbed regularly using a hard-bristle scrubbing brush, sunlight soap, a floor cloth and a pail of water. In Sherborne House the carpets and stairs were cleaned by maids on their knees, using a dustpan and brush. Maids and housewives inevitably tended to suffer from that common ailment, housemaids' knee.

The main method of travel in Victorian times was on foot (only the gentry, farmers and the clergy had the means to afford a horse to ride, or the luxury of a gig, trap or carriage in which to travel). Consequently, the stone roads and pavements proved very hard on footwear, which were most precious items, as they were very difficult and costly to replace. This was evinced in the following report by the head teacher entered in his log book in April 1897: 'One girl has only attended school five times out of a possible twenty-eight; she has been kept at home as her boots were worn out'.

All the cottages had outdoor privies and it was usually the responsibility of the man of the house to dispose of the contents into a pit in the garden. It was a common sight to see a hole dug in readiness for this operation but, when the garden was fully planted in the spring, positioning of such holes became more difficult. The task was completed primarily at night, or in the early hours of the morning.

Monday, the weekly washing day, was the most exacting day for any housewife. The copper, which was a fixture in the corner of the back kitchen or in an outside building, along with the tin bath and many other receptacles, had to be filled with water carried in from the pumps or wells. Another source of water was the ever-present rainwater butt. This not only reduced the distance the water had to be carried, but also provided much softer water which obtained a better lather and used less soap. Rainwater was also used for washing hair as it left a healthy sheen.

The fire in the copper was lit at the earliest opportunity on Monday morning, because a considerable time would pass before the water was hot enough to commence the washing. While the water was heating the clothes were sorted into separate piles; starting with the whites, sheets, pillowcases, tablecloths, aprons (worn by the majority of women and all young girls) and men's white shirt-collars. The coloureds were sorted according to their soiled condition, with socks and stockings generally coming last. Once the water had reached boiling point the clothes were placed in the copper, for about ten to fifteen minutes, filling the room with steam and the aroma of soap.

When the requisite time had elapsed, a stout wooden copper stick was used to haul the garments out and place them on the upturned copper lid, thereby allowing the clothes to drain and cool sufficiently enough to handle. Each item was then rinsed at least twice; once in a bath of clear water, then in another vessel containing blue water, coloured by squeezing out a Reckitt's blue bag (this process was used to 'enhance the whiteness' of the laundry). Each piece was then wrung through the mangle or wringer to remove excess water and finally hung out on the washing line to dry. The washing lines strung down some garden paths are, today, the only remaining links with those 'back-breaking' washing days of yore.

The white linen tablecloths, aprons, shirt-collars and any other item that required the process, were starched before being hung on the clothes line. This was accomplished by bathing the garments in a clear liquid obtained from mixing a small quantity of Colmans starch powder with a little cold water into a pastelike

Mr W. Tremaine and his daughter, in the early 1900s.

consistency, then adding sufficient boiling water. The starched items, when dry, required dampening with a little drop of cold water before being rolled up to await ironing. A large family wash could often take a whole day to complete.

The next time-consuming and arduous task was the ironing. This was carried out on the kitchen table, covered with an old blanket or horse rug and topped with a discarded sheet. Flat irons, heated on the top of the kitchen range or more commonly on a bracket suspended by hooks from the bars above the open fire, even during the hottest of days, were used. The invention of the primus stove proved an invaluable and time-saving aid in heating the flat iron. It was necessary to use a padded 'holder' to handle the hot irons which required rubbing down with a cloth, each time they were heated, in order to remove any ash or smoke-smuts. It was a rather tricky job to avoid getting burned during this process. A disgusting but common method used to test the temperature of the iron was to spit on it; if the spittle left the iron rapidly they were ready for use and, one trusted, not so hot as to scorch the clothing.

The laces, on babies' bonnets and maids' cap and aprons, were crimped using hot 'goffer' irons. To complete the ironing without some mishap was quite an art, or perhaps a stroke of luck, because extremely hot irons were utilized to smooth the creases of starched items.

A farmer's wife usually had a woman in from the village to help with the laundry. Sherborne House had, adjoining the stable block situated to the rear of the premises, a laundry complex where three ladies were employed as full-time laundry maids. This occasioned them living on the upper floors and carrying out their tasks on the ground floor. Racks attached to pulleys were used for indoor drying, while outside, a network of washing lines strung around the area of grass achieved the same purpose.

If one wonders why Sherborne House needed three full-time laundry maids, an inventory, taken in 1911, revealed what linen was deemed necessary for the day-to-day running of the house. A certain number of items were allocated to each department, which included the bedrooms and gentlemen's dressing rooms, the servants' bedrooms, servants' hall, stillroom (where the fancy cakes and pastrys were made), butler's pantry, housemaids' room, laundry, kitchen, stable block, gardeners' bothy and finally the dairy. Every item was marked in red cotton, with the letter 'S' (for Sherborne) surmounting a coronet, and the date of purchase. The total quantity required for the household comprised:

    206 pairs of sheets
    160 pillowcases
    690 towels (bath, round and huckleback)
    139 tableclothes
    261 glass and tea cloths
    576 table napkins
    284 doyleys
    402 dusters
     61 knifebox cloths,

plus aprons, counterpanes, blankets and all the Dutton family's personal washing.

Some of the tablecloths and napkins were dated 1861, towels 1863 and sheets 1894 – all evidently made from hard-wearing material.

A considerable change took place in the lifestyle of Lord and Lady Sherborne, following their departure to Windrush Manor at the outbreak of the Second World War. The greatest change was the sudden depletion in their household staff necessitating help from the women of the village on a daily basis.

The laundry at Sherborne House was retained for personal use, with the washing and ironing being completed by two or three local women on approximately three days in the week. A list follows of some of the women who undertook this task over the years:

Mrs Goodhall
Mrs Adams
Mrs W. Hayward
Mrs B. Large
Miss Mary Holtham
Mrs J. Pitts
Mrs V. Hayward
Mrs M. Hanks

Mrs L. Hooper and Mrs Sallis were the last two ladies to work the Sherborne House laundry. Mr Tom Stocks, who was employed at Windrush Manor, transported the laundry to and from Sherborne.

When the military vacated Sherborne House at the end of the Second World War, several local women were employed to clean the house in preparation for occupancy by the staff and pupils of King's School. The water used for this cleaning was heated in the laundry coppers and carried to the house. Due to the size of Sherborne House, as it contained several staircases and innumerable corridors and rooms, Mary Holtham informed me that the ladies would mark their way around using chalk, for fear of getting lost.

On occupation of the house, by King's School, the laundry ladies undertook the extra responsibility of washing the boys' socks! The bed linen and other items of clothing were sent to a local laundry.

In the cottages, the wash-house substituted as the bathroom once one became too old to bathe in front of the kitchen fire. Water, heated in the copper, was emptied into a zinc or tin bath which was placed on a rug on the floor. For warmth, a curtain was drawn across the door and the fire lid was opened. A candle or hurricane lamp provided the light and, having made the place as snug as possible, one could splash away quite happily – but it was certainly not a place in which to linger.

In between baths the families washed in their bedrooms, where a washstand, holding a wash basin, a large jug full of cold water (rainwater for preference), a soap dish and toothbrush holder, was kept for this purpose. Jugs or cans of hot water, heated on the kitchen fire, were carried upstairs. The ladies could wash down as far as possible, up as far as possible, and finally wash 'possible', so that cleanliness was maintained.

Lighting a fire in the bedrooms, which were seldom ever heated except in the case of severe illness, could be quite a perilous operation as furniture was often placed dangerously close to the small, open grate contained usually in just the one bedroom. Because of this, in the mornings during the winter months when the weather was particularly cold and frosty, the water in the jug on the washstand was often topped with a thin film of ice, especially if placed near the window where cold air was always seeping through the iron frames.

Beds were warmed by copper warming pans containing hot coals, stone bottles filled with hot water or with firebricks heated in the ovens and wrapped with several layers of old blanket.

With the installation of electricity in the cottages, mansions and buildings, plus modernization and mains water, and the ever improving electrical appliances and gadgets, life for the housewife and her family has been completely revolutionized in a relatively few years.

Dress too has changed dramatically over the years. Our grandmothers and forebears wore long dresses, mostly in black or grey, or some other sombre colour, down to their ankles. Wide-brimmed hats, profusely trimmed with feathers or silk flowers and secured to the hair by several long hatpins, were worn on the occasions they went out, even when they were working in the fields, helping the menfolk with the harvesting or haymaking. On the sabbath, a feather boa cape may be draped around the shoulders, button boots worn on the feet and a rolled umbrella clutched in the hands that were always covered by gloves, especially when attending church.

The aforementioned Mrs Saysome wore a long black skirt down to her ankles and a coarse sacking apron, tied around her waist, topped off with a man's cloth cap. On Sundays the sacking apron would be exchanged for a clean, white, starched one. On a warm sunny day she could be seen sitting on a wooden kitchen chair outside her front door. The children, who treated her with awe, likened her to a witch, especially as she always used herbal remedies for aches and pains in preference to doctors' medicines.

Our grandfathers wore stiff, starched, white collars attached to the shirt by studs. An alternative was a woollen crocheted front, worn over the shirt and fastened at the back by a button. Bowler hats were worn on Sundays, or for weddings and funerals, and the inevitable boots covered the feet. Agricultural workers often wore a corn sack, opened up one seam, cornerways over the head and shoulders for extra warmth and protection against the elements.

What a difference six decades have made! It would have been impossible to predict the changes of the last sixty years which now make life and labour so very much more bearable and happy. We take all this modernization for granted – until there is an electricity failure when we suddenly find ourselves in dire straits as we no longer possess the wherewithal to cope with life as it was lived in 'the good old days'.

CHAPTER NINE

Community Life

Because the village was part of a large estate, there was usually sufficient work for most of the male population, even as late as the 1930s. The men were employed in various roles ranging from tradesmen and labourers, whose job it was to maintain the estate, to shepherds and ploughmen working on the tenanted farms. There was thus little need to look elsewhere for work.

Because of this situation, and the fact that the majority of the villagers seldom ventured further than the local inn or beyond the parish boundary, the majority of marriages were between fellow cottagers and to the exclusion of outsiders. The result of this was an extensive interrelation among the villagers, thereby ensuring a tightly-knit community, so common in years gone by.

A positive side effect of this situation was the instant availability of helping hands among the many relatives living nearby, and the problem of finding assistance in the case of illness or the rearing of children was not a problem.

'New blood' was introduced through the hiring of outside servants for the big house and new families moving in to take up employment on the farms.

Prior to the twentieth century, it was the custom to hire agricultural workers and domestic servants at 'hiring fairs' and 'Mops'. These employment fairs were held at Stow-on-the-Wold, Burford and Cirencester. To enable those workers seeking employment to be easily distinguishable among the crowd, the maid servants wore a mob cap or carried either a mop or broom, the shepherd attached sheepswool to his hat, the carter would tie a piece of whipcord to his lapel and the cowman would try a similar ploy using cowhair. The prospective employers and the participants in these fairs would make their journeys by whatever means were available, the more affluent travelling on horseback or by horse and trap, while the less well off would walk, with the inns along the route providing welcome rest stops.

The local inn for Sherborne was the New Barn Inn (closed in the early 1920s), situated on the Ridgeway (A40), outside the village.

An unnamed writer/traveller, who had journeyed from the eastern counties in 1768, wrote, 'The road from Witney to Northleach is the worst turnpike I have ever travelled, a scandal to the country around. The stone which rises in vast flakes is used alone in pieces as large as one's head, a barbarous method.'

Opposite the New Barn Inn stood a turnpike lodge. The travellers, having to stop to pay their toll, were glad to enter the inn to rest awhile and enjoy the comforts of the establishment. A pint of best ale or porter and a hunk of bread and cheese costing around 3d., in the late nineteenth-century, could be consumed while drying oneself by the roaring log fire and gossiping with the locals. Travellers undertaking long journeys were pleased to rest their horses here and, if necessary, to have them reshod by the local blacksmith (these establishments were perhaps the forerunners of the modern motorway service stations).

Leslie Hayward recalls assisting in the dismantling of the dilapidated turnpike lodge, which had been constructed using carefully cut Cotswold stone. These stones were valuable for re-use by local builders, so great care was taken in a stone by stone dismantling process. Leslie recollects that he was unlucky in breaking some of the stones and was prepared to suffer the wrath of his employer, Mr W.H. Cook, but fortunately all was forgiven ('accidents will happen').

As there was no delivery of a daily newspaper and telephones had yet to be invented, it was left up to the village carrier to bring in news of the happenings in the outside world. Housewives could be seen, standing in their front doorways broom in hand or babe in arms with, quite often, another toddler clinging to their skirts, exchanging news and gossip with their neighbours. Men would do their gossiping (for they gossip just as much as the women) leaning over their garden gate or wall, or at the water pump when fetching buckets of water.

The villagers were able to keep few secrets from their neighbours, and what was not known first hand was soon to be found out, usually with a little spice added for good measure, by listening to the gossip, ''cause ther was allus summat a goin' on in them days, I can tell ee'.

If one of the men had lingered too long while partaking in a gossip session, his parting shot would probably have been, 'Well I must be a gettin' on 'ome or the missus 'll be wonderin' what's become of I'.

Children's pocket money would be earned by running errands to the shop or post

The first cascade, cow park and narrow water, 1877.

office, baby minding, or by fetching milk or water. Boys would often help out on the local farms to earn their pennies. Margaret Mate recalls that she was found work in the fields on Stones Farm in the early 1900s. Mr Stratton also provided work for Fred Margetts, pulling thistles at 1d. a hundred, or 1s. a day for cutting them down, and 6d. for helping his father clean out the cattle sheds on Saturdays and Sundays.

Another way to earn a penny was by opening and shutting gates for Mr Tremaine as he rode his horse around his farm. This was accomplished by riding behind Mr Tremaine and dismounting whenever a gate was encountered. William Tremaine stated that there were occasions when his grandfather trotted his horse along to the school to find a boy willing to carry out this service; the Margett boys were frequent recipients of his pennies.

A number of children, from both ends of the village, collected milk from the dairy situated to the rear of Sherborne House. During the early part of the twentieth century the dairy was managed by two spinster sisters, the Misses Annie and Mary Smith. Margaret Mate remembers that 'the dairy was officially open from 7 a.m. to 8 a.m., if anyone arrived late they found the door locked and consequently they had to wait in the yard while the two ladies finished their breakfast. As it was unheard of to return home empty handed, the inevitable result was to arrive late for school, thereby incurring the wrath of the headmaster, a situation not to be often repeated.'

Following the departure of the two Miss Smiths, Mr and Mrs Hubberd took up residence in the cottage (now used as the estate office). Mr Hubberd succeeded Harry Taylor as the electrician to Sherborne House. The electricity was supplied by

The lower waterfall by the turbine, early 1900s. Mr H. Taylor is standing on the bridge.

means of a turbine engine, powered by a water wheel. The 'turbine', as it was called, was situated by the side of the lower waterfall, and was accessible from the village street by a path leading past Dairy Farm and down alongside the wood. The route was lined with holly trees, old-fashioned roses and other shrubs, all of which combined to make a very picturesque setting. Alas, the turbine house is now in ruin; the planks of wood, placed across the narrow water channels, are now very rotten or gone altogether as too are the lovely shrubs and roses.

Mrs Hubberd managed the dairy and all that it entailed. Bread was baked twice weekly and cream was churned daily to make fresh butter for the dining table of the Big House. The footman collected the fresh milk, clotted cream and butter each morning, and delivered them to the house.

When the Hubberds left in about 1935, Charlie Lane moved into Dairy Farm and Mrs Hughes and daughter into Dairy Cottage. Kathleen, Mrs Hughes's daughter, practised hairdressing in a rented room in Northleach during the 'Marcel waving' period, before perms came into being. While a resident in Sherborne she entered and won a beauty competition, and was photographed in a bath with a sponge covering her modesty.

Miss Hanson and Miss Leach succeeded Mrs Hughes at the dairy, and remained there until its closure. Charlie Lane milked the herd of Jersey cows twice daily; the milk was emptied into a churn (resembling an oversized milk can), which was fixed to a metal frame on two large, solid-tyred wheels, and then wheeled several hundred yards to the dairy where the milk was decanted into large zinc pans (a deep groove was worn into the dairy flagstones where the churn was manoeuvred to the

The 'turbine' in the early 1900s.

waiting pans). Around this time Jersey milk cost 3d. per pint and skimmed milk 1½d.

At the Top End of the village Mrs Broad and her son Arnold supplied and delivered milk and fresh eggs (costing 1s. per dozen in the 1920s and most certainly free range) daily to the cottagers. A truck was used to transport the milk churn to the village, where the contents were ladled into milk cans or jugs at the cottage door.

Maggie Saunders, an octogenarian, recalls, 'Arnold carried a scythe to cut the grass along the side of the road to supplement the feed for their cows, as they were short of grazing land'. When Mrs Broad died Arnold ceased the delivery to concentrate on his smallholding at Ducklestone Mill. He later married the district nurse and moved to Upper Slaughter.

Mrs Saunders can also remember the occupants of Ducklestone Mill prior to the Broads. They were millers, by the name of Howard, who made bread which they delivered around the village. They had one daughter, a lovely girl called Nellie, who was the first child to ride a bicycle to school. Mr Reg Pinchin, from Aldsworth, took over the Broads' customers when Arnold stopped his delivery.

At the Bottom End of the village, Mr William Tremaine was doing his own delivery of milk and eggs using a pony and trap. His customers were required to take their jugs and cans out to his churn, on the trap in the street. When he changed to bottle delivery, the bottles were stacked into a wooden truck and Mr Tremaine employed Mrs Elizabeth Saunders to take on the round. After many years Mrs Saunders was succeeded by Maria Newport who, with a happy smiling face, delivered the latest news and gossip seven days a week, along with the daily 'pinta'. Saturday, 7 October 1961 was the final delivery day for Mrs Newport and the end of the Tremaines' village delivery, as it became a requirement for all milk to be pasteurized before sale to the public. Mr Norman, of Bourton-on-the-Water, had already taken over Mr Pinchin's round, and Sunday 8 October 1961 heralded his delivery to the whole village. Miss Nora Weaving, who lived with her sister Mrs Preston Senior at Home Farm, faithfully met Mr Norman by the war memorial every morning to collect her milk, come rain or shine.

Other companies that delivered milk in the village included the Co-op, Quinneys and Elm Farm Dairies. Today, Clifford Dairies supply the daily pinta, delivered by Terry Hooper who was born at Top End, as were his father and grandfather. Old Mr Hooper, Terry's grandfather, worked in the gardens of Sherborne House until his retirement, after which he worked two days a week in 'The Cottage' garden for the Hon. George Dutton.

The families living in the lodges outside the village had to rely on tins of condensed milk for daily use (while the village housewife usually kept a tin for emergencies only). Condensed milk was much enjoyed by the children, either spread on a slice of bread or by the spoonful straight from the tin.

There was a period, during the early part of the twentieth century, when Lady Ethel Sherborne gave a Christmas party for all the school children, held each year in the servants' hall. The long trestle tables would groan under the weight of food; sandwiches, buns, cakes, an assortment of jellies and trifles, and a Christmas cracker for each child. The footmen, looking resplendent in their fawn-coloured

Empire Day celebrations in the late 1920s. Back row, left to right: Mrs L. Larner, Mrs W. Stevens, Mrs E. Johnson, Mrs J. Clark, Mrs Hooper. Middle row: Phyllis Wilsdon, Gladys Petrie, Mrs Joy, Edna Hicks, Mrs W. Hayward, Eileen Larner, Mrs B. Larner, Dorothy Stevens, Mrs Hill, Winnie Jones, Muriel Lester, Eileen Larner. Front row: Mrs Houlton, Mrs Lane, Mrs Cambray.

uniforms with red waistcoats, waited on all present. After the meal, when the tables were cleared and stacked away, games were organized; one of the favourites being 'pinning on the donkey's tail'. Following the games came a cinematograph show of Charlie Chaplin films, organized by the Hon. Charles (later to become Lord Sherborne) and the Hon. George Dutton. Lady Sherborne and her two daughters, Miss Pamela and Miss Juliet, were always in attendance. Lord Sherborne, however, was always absent (very rarely would he take part in any of the village social activities). A very enjoyable party was closed with a vote of thanks from Mr Demer echoing to 'three cheers' from the children, and the evening would conclude with Lady Sherborne presenting each child with an orange and a bag of sweets (a real treat).

The Sherborne and Windrush Horticultural Show, an annual event which involved the majority of the local community, was founded in the nineteenth century and held in the grounds of Sherborne Park, by kind permission of Lord Sherborne. A schedule for the show held on Wednesday 6 August 1919 (kindly loaned by Mrs Dorothy Stevens), states that it was the twenty-eighth annual show. The following were principals:

President   Rt. Hon. Lord Sherborne

Vice-Presidents Major J.H. Dutton
                 A.L. Davis Esq.

G.F. Moor JP
W.A. Rixon JP
Revd J.G.D. Willis

Men's Committee:
Chairman   R. Gray

Vice-Chairman   R.F. Stratton

Members:

H.H. Demer	Thos. Dow
A. Cook	W.H. Blake
Chas. Pratley	R. Barber
A. Tye	Thos. Matthews
M. James	James Taylor
H. Taylor	Thos. Lester
F.J. Blake	H. Paget
D. Large	E. Guest
A. Petrie	Geo. Phillips
Thos. Mumford	W. Stevens
W. Tremaine	J. Whitehead

Ladies Committee:
President   Mrs Corbett
Members: The Lady Alice Havelock Allen
                  The Lady Eleanor Bying
                  Mrs Willis   Mrs Dow
                  Mrs Demer   Miss Tremaine
                  Mrs James   Nurse Gardiner
                  Mrs Matthews (Windrush)
                  Mrs Matthews (Sherborne)
                  Mrs Speke

Honourable Secretary and Treasurer:
         A. Mitchell (gardener to Lord Sherborne)

Admission to the show was 1s. from 2 p.m. to 4 p.m., 6d. after 4 p.m. Children half price (a reduction if more than three children to one family).
Sports commenced at 5 p.m. sharp, with dancing 6.30 p.m. to 10 p.m. There were three classes for exhibitors:

Class A – Amateurs and Gardeners
Class B – Artisans
Class C – Cottagers.

There were twenty-one entries for exhibits in all three classes. Prize money was also the same in all classes:

1st Prize – 2s. 6d.

Villagers enjoying the entertainment at the Flower Show on the lawns of Sherborne House in 1913.

2nd Prize – 1s. 6d.
3rd Prize – 1s. 0d.
Entries were as follows:

    (1) Three cauliflowers
    (2) Three cabbages
    (3) Twenty scarlet runner beans
    (4) Twenty pods of broad beans
    (5) Twenty pods of peas
    (6) Eight kidney beans
    (7) Eight round potatoes
    (8) Two vegetable marrows
    (9) Eight onions (white or straw coloured)
    (10) Dish of twenty eschalots (separate bulbs)
    (11) Six carrots
    (12) $\frac{1}{2}$ lb blackcurrants
    (13) $\frac{1}{2}$ lb red currants (to be shown in bunches)
    (14) $\frac{1}{2}$ lb white currants (in bunches)
    (15) Twenty-four white gooseberries
    (16) Twenty-four red gooseberries
    (17) Three pot plants (in or out of bloom)
    (18) Three ports of balsam (three varieties)
    (19) Four varieties of carnations (two blooms of each)
    (20) Four varieties of stocks (one plant of each to be shown as cut flowers)
    (21) Collection of sweet peas (eight varieties, arranged separately with own foliage)

OPEN CLASSES A, B & C.

    (1)   Collection of garden flowers, to be arranged for effect, stand not to exceed 6 ft 6 ins x 2 ft
    (2)   Collection of vegetables, six different varieties
    (3)   Collection of fruit, six kinds, and not more than one variety of a kind
    (4)   African marigolds, six blooms
    (5)   Basket of flowers, arranged for effect (ladies only)
    (6)   Hand bouquet (ladies only)
    (7)   Six distinct varieties of garden flowers, arranged separately with own foliage
    (8)   Six distinct varieties of asters, one bloom of each
    (9)   Brace of cucumbers
    (10)   Six beetroot
    (11)   Six turnips
    (12)   Eight onions, red or purple
    (13)   Six leeks
    (14)   Messrs Garne offer a prize for the best eight onions, separate dish
    (15)   Dish of cooked potatoes

Sherborne Senior School children displaying the winning Bird and Tree Shield in 1924. Standing, left to right: I. Larner, R. Walker, S. Larner, M. Cyphus (pupil teacher), –?–, R. Pitts, L. Shepherd, –?–, V. Panter, D. Shepherd, V. Hill, M. Morse, D. Petrie, A. Margetts, W. Petrie. Front row: M. Lester, G. Petrie, K. Smith, R. Saysome.

(16)   A prize in kind for the best dish of culinary apples. 2nd prize 2s., 3rd prize 1s.

(17)   A prize in kind for the best dish of dessert apples. 2nd prize 2s., 3rd prize 1s.

(18)   A prize in kind for the best three heads of celery.

(19)   A prize in kind for the best collection of salad (no second or third prize for entry nos 18 and 19)

AGRICULTURAL PRODUCE

(20)   Best dish of eight hen's eggs from cottagers poultry only

(21)   Best 1 lb of run honey

(22)   Best two sections of honey

(23)   Messrs James Carter & Co., Seedsmen, gave three prizes to the exhibitors showing the best results of exhibits from produce from their seeds

(24)   Special prizes offered by Messrs John Jefferies & Sons Ltd, Cirencester, for collection of vegetables of six kinds grown from their seeds

(25)   Special prizes offered by Mr Neal, Seedsman of Bourton-on-the-Water, for a dish of eight Majestic potatoes, a dish of eight Great Scott potatoes and for a dish of eight Lochar potatoes grown from their seed [Mr Neal used to sell seed around the village].

SCHOOL CHILDREN'S CLASS: (open to both parishes [Windrush had its own school then])

(26)   Collection of wild flowers by girls
(27)   Collection of wild flowers by boys
(28)   Best made hand-work model
(29)   Best crayon or painting from nature (open to boys and girls)
(30)   Best drawing to scale, by boys
(31)   Collection of queen wasps (school children only) to be taken to the headmaster by 30 June 1919

NEEDLEWORK (open to both parishes)

(32)   Best made children's knickers or chemise (Standard V or VI)
(33)   Best made child's pinafore or overall (Standards III and IV)

KNITTING (open to both parishes)

(34)   Best pair of knitted gloves (Standard VI)
(35)   Best pair of men's socks (Standard V). All needlework to be done in school under the supervision of the teacher. Work not to be taken home
(36)   Best cultivated plot in Sherborne School garden
(37)   Best collection of vegetables grown on plot (there is a fourth prize of 6d. for all the school children's classes)

SPECIAL PRIZES (open to both parishes)

(38)   Give by Mrs Basil Corbett. For the best cut-out and made garment, by a girl attending school. 1st prize. 3s., 2nd prize 2s., 3rd prize 1s.
(39)   Given by the Hon. Mrs Charles Dutton. For the best marking in red cross-stitch in capital and small letters, alphabetically and roman and plain figures. Materials will be supplied (a 4th prize of 6d.)
(40)   Given by Lady Eleanor Byng. For the best set of clothes for baby (nainsook or cambric frock, flannel barracoat and knitted vest). Prizes 3s., 2s. and 1s.

Phew! What a schedule!

Fred Margetts won four third prizes at this show, however this was a long way from the achievement of his father; five First prizes, three Seconds and two Thirds at this same show.

It would have required a large marquee to display all of these exhibits, and considerable time in preparation for the exhibitors. The horticulture show schedules of today are much less demanding. (Today it would be extremely difficult to find twenty runner beans of near equal length, for example, as garden produce is no longer grown in such large quantities as in the past.)

In the past it was necessary to plant large quantities of vegetables, as there were many more mouths to feed than in the present-day family. The idea of having to purchase vegetables (even if it were possible) would have been an anathema or as a result of a disaster, since everyone took great pride in their gardens and gardening skills. Neighbours were always generous in sharing their surplus produce, as indeed some are today.

Each house was allotted a large garden (much too large in many cases today) and some supplemented this area with an allotment rented from the estate. In addition to this, farm employees were able to plant one or two rows of potatoes, according to their requirements, when the farmer planted his crops.

It was a common sight to see a villager walking along the street on the way to his allotment, with his gardening tools either slung over his shoulder, or lying in a wheelbarrow. The village lads, much to their dismay, had to give of their services for an hour or so, to help with the digging or planting, before meeting up with their sweethearts or joining their pals for a kick about with a football. A group of stately elm trees (opposite Numbers 45 and 46, long since removed) or the shelter of the huge sycamore tree, also removed, by the war memorial, were favourite meeting places for the village youngsters.

In addition to the displays of flora and produce at the horticultural show, there were also other attractions, one of which was a comic football match with the teams taking part in a fancy dress parade. One photograph (see p. 116) reveals the players in the following dress: a Red Indian squaw; Britannia; a clown; a suffragette; a 'Tommy'; a haymaker; a housewife; a mother with baby sucking a dummy in a pram; a gentleman with top hat etc. Enquiries have failed to produce any literature or photographs of any horticultural show after 1923, so presumably that was the date of the last show.

In recent years a local show has been revived; it is called the Windrush Valley Horticultural Show, and is held on the second Saturday in September in the barn at Windrush Manor. The show has a wide range of exhibits and only asks for five of a variety. It is interesting to note that the children's section comprises a fruit model, an edible necklace, a 6 in x 4 in birthday card of pressed flowers – nothing as demanding as a pair of knitted gloves or a baby's barracoat.

It would appear that the annual village fete took the place of the horticultural show, the first being held in August 1924 in the grounds of Sherborne House, the proceeds going towards church funds.

Throughout the 1920s and 1930s Mr Demer, the schoolmaster, played an important role in the organization of the fete. The usual competitions included 'bowling for a pig', the prize being donated by one of the local farmers. The first prize went to whoever obtained the highest score by bowling three balls into a circle of three rings marked out with chalk. The eventual winner often spent more than it would have cost to buy the pig, but there was always the excitement and thrill of trying to beat the person holding the highest score. Other attractions included a display of country dancing, made famous by Cecil Sharpe. The males also performed some of the morris dances. Another highlight was an open mixed tennis tournament held on three courts opposite the house. In later years, when they were old enough, the girls from Westwoods Grammar took part and would put up a reputable show.

Comedian 'Chick' Fowler hosted a concert party which came from Cheltenham. There were the usual side shows including a fortune teller, a bran tub, a hoop-la etc. Teas were supplied and a quantity of meat and fish-paste sandwiches, buns, scones, small cakes, and delicious ice cream made from real cream, all supplied by Lady Sherborne and made by her cook, was consumed.

When one tired of watching the events, or one's spending money was exhausted,

Fancy dress competitors and spectators at a Flower Show in the early 1900s.

Sherborne team of Folk and Morris Dancers in the middle 1920s. Back row, left to right: Mrs L. Margetts, Mrs F. Petrie, Mrs L. Larner, Mrs L. Cyphus, Nurse Hambling, Miss de la Hey (teacher), Miss D. Stevens, Mrs C. Cyphus, Mrs E. Johnson, Mr Earl (musician). Front row: –?–, Frank Stevens, Ern Saunders, Fred Stevens, Charlie Jones (jun.), Bill Hayward.

one could always explore the immaculate grounds. Weather permitting, the evening was concluded with dancing on the lawns.

The favourite day for the children was the Annual Club Day, which celebrated the forming of a Working Man's Benefit Club during the early 1900s, and was held on the Tuesday following Whitsunday.

A small sum of money, paid to the elected secretary treasurer, ensured that the working man's family would have the services of a doctor free, and a small weekly sick-payment should the husband fall ill.

Young girls would mark the day by wearing a new dress, usually white and, almost exclusively, made by mother. The children, all keyed up with excitement, would awake early on Club Day to await eagerly the arrival of the show people who would set up their side shows in the field behind the village school. Two Burford families did the rounds of the clubs; the Forest family would bring swinging boats, roundabouts and coconut shies, while the Bowerman family sold toys, cuddly teddy bears, monkeys on sticks etc.

The villagers would congregate on Tremaine's Corner, at the Bottom End, from 10.30 a.m. About 11.00 a.m. the Chedworth Silver Band, headed by Daniel Large carrying the Union Jack banner, led the procession to the church, where a short service conducted by the local vicar was held. After the service, the band led the procession back to the war memorial, where the vicar said a short prayer before everyone dispersed.

Villagers with the Chedworth Band gathered around the war memorial on Club Day, 1928.

The males would then proceed into the school to partake of a lunch of cold salt beef, potatoes, pickled onions and chutney, followed by cheese, all washed down with glasses of beer, or lemonade, made from fresh lemons, for the young lads. This repast was prepared by the village WI ladies, the men only had to provide their cutlery, glass and a plate.

The females made their way home, to have a bite, before leaving to explore the fairground.

By mid afternoon the field events were in full swing; screams and shrieks of laughter came from the swinging boats, where the men tried to outdo each other by swinging their boat higher than that of their neighbour, while trying to impress their female companions. The coconut shies would do a roaring trade; it was very difficult to dislodge these coconuts from their cups.

The candy stalls sold 'spit rock', so called because it was made from equal quantities of brown and white paste stretched and plaited together, and it was not unknown for the person making it to spit on their hands occasionally during the production! Once it set it was broken with the aid of a small wooden mallet, weighed on a set of scales (these scales had a shallow pan on one side, to contain the substance to be weighed, and a flat plate on the other upon which the weights were placed), before being emptied into a poke bag.

One could always purchase a bag of broken ice-cream wafers and locust bean pods for a ha'penny ($\frac{1}{2}$d.). Locust bean pods were normally used as animal feed, but they were very popular when used in the aforesaid manner.

Other attractions included bowling for a pig (as mentioned earlier), skittles for a case of beer, the ladies could win a tea service (in the same manner as the men, when bowling for a pig), running races, three-legged races and sack races. As the field had been occupied by a herd of cows prior to this wonderful day, it was almost impossible to set out the course to avoid all the cow pats that 'mined' the field, so inevitably a few unfortunate souls had to have a cleaning session afterwards.

Chedworth bandsmen, whose repertoire included all the popular tunes, continued to play throughout the afternoon in direct competition to the hurdy-gurdy organ on the roundabout, the shrieks and screams of those enjoying themselves, and the cries from the stall holders to 'come and try your luck'. It was no wonder that occasionally the bandsmen would slip away to the beer tent to slake their thirst. Some of the ladies were also occasional visitors to the beer tent; one in particular was Mrs Parrott who wore the most outrageous hats profusely trimmed with feathers, often bright mauve in colour. By the end of the day she was usually 'one over the eight' and was often found the following morning in the cemetery, lying by her husband's grave.

After all the trestle tables had been cleared from serving tea throughout the day, dismantled and stacked outside for eventual return to their normal storage place in the stableyard, the festivities were concluded with a dance in the schoolroom. Over the years the variety of dances included the minuet, the mazurka, quadrilles, the gavotte, lancers, the veleta, the Paul Jones, the Charleston, the waltz, foxtrot, two step, polka, and the tango. On 7 February 1908 an invitation dance was held in the school, and as it warranted a mention in the school logbook, was probably the first dance to be held there.

Children's races, Sherborne Club in 1914.

These festive days are always remembered as being gloriously happy, with clear blue skies and lots of sunshine, but in 1910 a very severe thunderstorm brought the outdoor activities to a precipitous end. This event prompted the following report in the headmaster's logbook, 'A severe thunderstorm occurred at night and panic took place. One woman had an epileptic fit until about 11 p.m., and was attended to in the school. No less than five men (mostly drunk) had to be removed from the school premises.'

In between village events, the lads and lasses walked or cycled to Northleach and neighbouring villages. For the young ladies cycling was a tedious affair, as it was necessary to hitch up securely their long dance dresses, thus ensuring they remained clear of the spokes and cycle chain, but many dresses were still torn in the process.

Morris dancing, in evidence as far back as 1777, is a display of set dances, by six or eight fit and energetic men, and is always performed outdoors. There were several teams of dancers in the Cotswolds, some of the more local ones being Sherborne, Longborough, Bledington, Chipping Camden and Oddington, Little Barrington with Windrush and Bampton, all just over the border in Oxfordshire, also supported their own teams.

The dancing commenced at Whitsuntide, the Sherborne Morris danced in Sherborne on Whit Tuesday and then on and off for three weeks; reference has been made to them dancing in Milton and Shipton-under-Wychwood.

In those days the men danced to a whistle, about a foot in length, called variously a 'whittle and dub', 'tabor' or 'fife', accompanied by a small, flat drum hung on the

The Lady Helpers of Sherborne Club photographed on 25 May 1920. Back row, left to right: Mrs J. Larner, –?–, Miss N. Pittaway, –?–, Miss G. Larner. Middle row: Mrs C. Larner, Mrs L. Cambray, –?–, Mrs B. Larner, Mrs D. Large, Mrs Joy. Front row: Miss G. Jones, Miss D. Stevens, Mrs W. Stevens, Mrs T. Dow, –?–, Mrs T. Mathews, Mrs Pratley.

performer's finger and beaten with a short drumstick. In more recent years, music has been supplied by a melodeon, fiddle/violin or accordion. The man in charge of the dancers carried the collecting box and generally acted as the fool. He would carry a stick to which was tied an inflated pig's bladder at one end and the tail of an animal at the other, and the stick was flourished to keep the spectators at bay. The fool, who also entertained the onlookers by relating jokes, was the only member of the team to receive a wage – the idea behind this was that he would remain sober, thereby able to keep the team together, as traditionally, vast quantities of ale would be quaffed by the thirsty dancers.

It was quoted, 'Sherborne was a desperate Morris place!'. The nineteenth-century dancers' dress consisted of a white shirt, deeply pleated back and front, white knee breeches, blue stockings and a 'Billy Cock' hat (square, high, black hat) trimmed with coloured ribbons. A diagonal sash was suspended across the right shoulder, while pads of twenty-five bells (five rows of five) were strapped just below the knees. For most dances each man carried a large handkerchief, tied with a reef knot to the little finger, thereby leaving the hands free to clap. They danced in 'the lightest shoes obtainable' (specially acquired for the purpose).

The performers danced on to the display area in single file, then around the enclosure, finally forming up in the centre, for the dance. On concluding their display, they departed in serpentine fashion, making their obeisance by pulling a forelock.

Committee Members of Sherborne Club, 1924–5. Standing, left to right: W. Tremaine, L. Cyphus, –?–, W. Johnson, W. Harding, R.F.C. Stratton, A. Jones, F. Taylor, A. Hill, A. Mills, C. Larner, E. Margetts. Seated: D. Large, Revd G. Warner, A. O'Reilly, D. Renn, T. Mathews, Mr Ing. Seated, front: R. Saunders, L. Hemmings.

Sherborne Morris had three types of dances:

(1)   set dances, in which all six men dances, more or less continuously;
(2)   corner dances, requiring diagonally opposing pairs to change places in turn;
(3)   jigs, dances as solos or duets.

The Sherborne dances were named as follows:

(1)   Lads abunching;
(2)   Cuckoo's nest;
(3)   Old woman tossed up in a blanket;
(4)   Constant Billie, the only stick dance, with sticks 18 inches long and less than 1 inch in diameter (in the olden days they were painted red, white and blue);
(5)   Monks' march;
(6)   Miss Trinkles;
(7)   Young Collins;
(8)   I'll go and enlist for a sailor;
(9)   My Lord Sherborne's jig;
(10)   Orange and blue (or orange in bloom).

The Sherborne dance differed to that of other teams in that it was a step, hop and

'My Lord Sherborne's Morris Men' dancing on the hill at Bottom End, photographed in the late 1980s.

change, and was danced with arms outstretched. Named among the earliest morris dancers were: Thomas Kench, Thomas Pitts, George and James Simpson, Edward James, Albert Townsend and James (Jim) Larner. Charlie Jones danced with the Little Barrington and Windrush team before moving to Sherborne.

Research indicates that the old Sherborne Morris ceased in the late 1880s. It was not until the early part of the twentieth century that efforts were made by Cecil Sharpe to revive the morris. In doing so he interviewed Albert Townsend, the shopkeeper and postmaster, who was also interviewed by the travelling morris in 1924.

In 1978 morris dancing was again revived, this time by Barry Baker. The main source of information and teaching was Keith Chandler of Evesham, an historian on the subject, who contributes articles to the Gloucestershire Family History Society.

The team, calling themselves 'My Lord Sherborne's Morris Men', live locally. Two Sherborne lads, Andrew and Oliver Minns, joined the team for a brief period. The men dress as near as is possible in the traditional costume, but the breeches have been replaced by white trousers and the hat, although still trimmed with ribbons augmented with feathers and flowers, is a more shallow, black affair. The Sherborne Morris give a display of their dancing in the village at least once a year, usually on Whit Monday.

Another past form of entertainment, all but forgotten until recently, was that of the mummers play, acted by amateurs during the Christmas period. James M. Carpenter, an American folklorist, discovered versions of a text in a manuscript collection (microfilm in Vaughan Williams Memorial Library), while collecting material in Britain. Among the names mentioned as being the text informants were: William Bunting who was born in 1860, and his brother Thomas born 1862, both of whom had learned the play from their father, James, born 1832; Daniel Large, born 1865; Walter Souls, born 1865; and Thomas Saunders whose tutor was his brother who, in turn, had picked it up from his grandfather, Albert Hooper, born 1845. Over the ensuing years, other performers who will be remembered by the senior citizens are Jim Larner, Walter and Jim Matthews, Albert Cyphus, Fred Larner, Roland Harding, Cecil and Leslie Large, Ben and Teddy Williams, Ernest Souls and William Hayward.

The last time the play was performed was between 1934 and 1937. The actors during this period were Francis and Ernie Larner, Stuart Saunders, Charlie Stevens, Steve and Teddy Williams, with Teddy Margetts playing Father Christmas. The following is an abridged version of the play, reported by Jack Saunders in 1980, which has recently come to light:

A door is opened in response to knocking and Father Christmas *steps in.*
Father Christmas: Please to let the Mummers act.

In comes I old Hind-before, I come forrard to open the door.

In comes I old Father Christmas, welcome here or welcome not,

I hope old Father Christmas will never be forgot.

I brought a besom to sweep your house,

I brought a besom to kick up a dust.

I pray good Master and good Missus, I hope you're both within.

Sherborne mummers, Christmas 1913. From left to right: A. Cyphus (soldier), W. Matthews (Beelzebub), C. Large (Prussian King), Daniel Large (in cap), F. Larner (doctor), G. Saunders (Father Christmas), Jimmie Matthews (old woman), R. Harding, Jack Vinney.

I comes this merry Christmas time to show you kith and kin
And if you take it as offence, pray tell it unto me
And I will be quickly gone or hence.
A room, a room for my brave gallant men.
I come this merry Christmas time to show you activity
Activity of youth, activity of age,
I'll show you all the prettiest action you ever saw acted upon a common
stage.

David Brand *enters, recites his little bit and requests entry of the* King. *The*
King *enters and boasts of his prowess over the French, Spaniards or Turks;*

The King: I know there's no man here can do me a hurt,
  Mince pies hot, mince pies cold,
  I'd send him to Satan before he was nine days old.

Whereupon Father Christmas *calls in the valiant Soldier bold. A fight takes
place between the Soldier and the* King *who is knocked to the floor. The* Old
Woman, *who has entered unbidden, gestures with her broomstick and kneels to
attend to the* King. *The* Doctor *is called and speaks to Jack Finney.*

Doctor: Hold this'oss [horse].

Jack Finney: Hold 'im thiself.

Doctor: In comes I, bold Dr Ariel, very well known at home and abroad
  I've got some pills, they are but few,
  They'll search your body and stomach through.
  I've got some pills, they are the best,
  They'll cure North, South, East and West.
  And here bold fellow, there's one for you!

He bends down and gives the King *a pill.*

Father Christmas: Doctor, what else canst thee cure?

Doctor: All sorts of disease, just what my pills please.
  The itch, the stitch, the fits,
  the palsies, the gout,
  All pains within and all pains without.
  All bruises and sprains, all shopick stills without any grains.
  Bring any old woman to me,
  99 years of age or 99 years laid in her grave.
  If she'll rise up and crack one of my pills
  I'll bound her life to save.
  Moreover, I'll maintain, I'll break her neck and set'un again.

Eventually Beelzebub *enters:*

Beelzebub: In comes I old Beelzebub, on my shoulder I carries a club,
  In my hand a dripping pan, don't you think I a jolly old man?
  Last Christmas time as I turned the spit,
  I burnt me left finger and I felt it hit.
  The spark sped o'er the table, the pot lid beat the ladle,
  Aye aye, cried the gridiron, can't you two agree
  I'm the justice, just bring 'un to me.
  Down came the chimbley, down the frying pan with his long tail,

Sweared if he was the justice, he'd send them all to jail,
In farmers' time when pigs were swine
And birds used to build in Old Man's Beard,
That wasn't in my time – perhaps not in thine.
After more fighting followed by tomfoolery and wit, Jack Finney *makes his entrance.*
Jack Finney: In comes I as ain't been it,
  With my big head and little wit,
  My wit's so big, my head's so small,
  I'll play a tune to please you all.
They circle the room, singing.
All: Pray Master and Missus, come sit by the fire,
  Put your hand in your pocket I pray and desire.
  Put your hand in your pocket and pull out your purse
  A little of something you'll never think worse.
  Go down to your cellar and see what you'll find
  Your barrell's not empty if you will be kind.
  If you will be kind with a glass of good beer,
  We won't call upon you until the next year
  Sing father o'raddy, sing father o'raddy
  Sing father o'raddy aye aye.

For those males who were not interested, or were past taking part in energetic social activities, their spare time was spent in more rewarding pursuits such as pig or bee keeping. A pig club was formed in the village and each member paid an annual subscription of 6d. per pig, and competed for a cup. On registration, the pigs were inspected by a responsible person to ensure they were healthy. In the event of the death of the animal, through whatever causes, the owner was entitled to the current value or whatever amount happened to be in the kitty at the time.

Mr Andy O'Reilly, a painter on the estate but residing in Windrush, was club secretary, followed by Alan Hill, head keeper. Tom Matthews, chairman, was the recipient of the cup on three occasions, for having the best managed pig club in Gloucestershire. It was presented to him by Lord Bledisloe. In due course the pig would either have to be sold to a butcher or slaughtered locally, thereby supplying a generous quantity of meat to the family.

Quite a number of men kept hives of bees, and some of the names that come to mind are Jim Saunders and his sons (Jack, Fred and Tom), Alf Mills, Tom Shepherd, Jim Larner, Tom Matthews and Ern Johnson who used the old skip type of hive.

It is estimated that on average, there are 30,000 bees in a swarm. There is an old country rhyme, as follows:

> A swarm of bees in May is worth a load of hay,
> A swarm of bees in June is worth a silver spoon,
> But a swarm of bees in July isn't worth a butterfly.

Mr Tom Mathews with the Pig Club cup.

The honey proved a lucrative sideline for keepers brave enough to extract it from the hives. To provide some protection during the tricky operation of removing honey, the keeper would wear a fine muslin hood covering head and face, worn over a wide-brimmed hat, with long gloves to prevent the bees crawling up their sleeves. A pair of bellows, emitting some substance to make the bees docile, was inserted into the hive and the sections of honey were removed for sale in small sections or run off into 1 lb jars for storage. The local honey was consumed by the spoonful to stave off colds or sore throats, or was delicious when spread on a slice of bread and butter.

Mrs Margetts had her own special recipe, purported to have come from a gypsy, for a mixture for chesty coughs:

1 lb honey   1 pint of cod liver oil
the juice of two lemons   2 oz of spirits of camphor

Method: Mix all of the ingredients together in a large jug standing in a saucepan of hot water. DO NOT allow the mixture to boil. When thoroughly infused, pour into screw-top jars for storage. I can vouch that it is a very effective, but foul-tasting tincture. Jim Larner would call it 'Mrs Margett's miracle cure'.

Honey was also the main ingredient for making mead:

4 lbs honey	1 gallon water
1 oz yeast	

Method: Mix honey with water and boil for one hour, skim when lukewarm, add yeast and a little lemon peel (if desired). Cover and leave overnight in a warm place. Pour into a clean cask and leave to ferment as for wine.

Margaret Mate recalls that Sandy Pitts (who was employed on the estate to keep the drive, from Sherborne House to Cheltenham Lodges, clear from leaves and undergrowth) would put handfuls of bees under his arm saying that the stings were good for his rheumatism.

The following is a lovely letter written to a beekeeper:

> Would you cum over and 'ave a look at my son's bees 'cos he don't know
> whether there be a queen among 'em or not, and I thought you could give 'em
> a couple of puffs of smoke with that contraption of your'n and find out.
> P.S. Could you bring a queen along just in case there ain't one.

To my knowledge nobody in the village keeps bees at the present time, but Alf Mills's daughter Maidie and his grandson John Swallow run a successful import and export honey business in Witney.

In days gone by, bell ringing was a popular hobby for the male population, with change ringing of the bells always a joyful sound to hear. During the nineteenth century Charlie Jones was a member of the Gloucester and Bristol Diocesan Change Ringing Association for which he paid an annual subscription of 1s. 6d.

PERFORMING MEMBER'S RECEIPT.
WITH THANKS IN BEHALF OF THE ASSOCIATION.

From REV. PITT EYKYN,
ASHTON GATE, BRISTOL.

Gloucester & Bristol Diocesan Change Ringing Association.

No. 731   *Feb 12 1886*

Received of Mr C. Jones

the sum of One Shilling and Sixpence, for one
Year's subscription to the Association.

£0 1s. 6d.   Pitt Eykyn, Hon. Sec.

                              Pro. Treasurer.

Receipt for membership of Gloucester & Bristol Change Ringing Association, 1886.

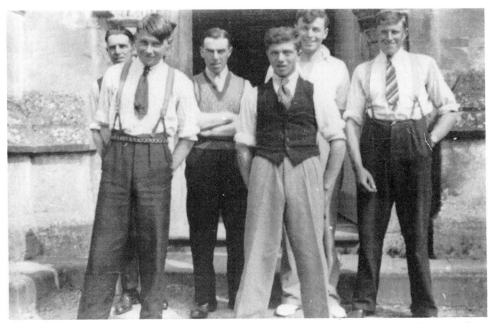

Bell-ringers in the late 1930s. Back row, left to right: Vic Dodson, Arthur Dodson, Bill Petrie, Stan Akerman. Front row: Norman Barrett and Fred Smith.

Sherborne always boasted a good team of bell ringers, and a pre-war photograph, probably of the last full team, is shown here.

There was also an excellent team of hand-bell ringers in the village during the early part of the nineteenth century, who performed in the villagers' homes during the Christmas period.

Regrettably, there are no longer any bell-ringers resident in the village. Harry Taylor, now living in Bourton-on-the-Water and still a church warden and Secretary to the PCC, will on occasion toll one bell when a service is to be held.

During the 1920s, Miss Hester Handy (housekeeper and sister-in-law to Mr R.F. Stratton) ran a Girls' Friendly Society for the young girls of the village. Meetings were held one evening a week in the drawing room at Stones Farm.

The village also fielded very successful cricket and football teams. The school also fared exceptionally well at football during Mr Demer's time as headmaster. Although the sports fields were some distance away from the village, there was always ample support, both male and female. The venue for sporting occasions was the Park near the Cheltenham Lodges, either side of the stately avenue of beech trees. Cricket was played on the side on which the pavilion stands, with football on the opposite side. During their occupation of Sherborne House, King's School took over the football pitch, subsequently the villagers used the pavilion side for both sports.

Water, required by the footballers to wash themselves or to make tea and glasses of lemonade, had to be carried from one of the lodges and heated on an oil or primus stove.

Sherborne Rovers, 1947/8. Back row, left to right: Mr Herrin, Lionel Cambray, Ernie Larner, Harry Taylor, Leslie Hayward, Walter Tufnell, David Margetts. Middle row: Ron Hayward, P.C. Reynolds, Michael Howard. Front row: Bill Maunders, Bill Moore, Eric Saunders, Henry Shepherd, Donald Saunders.

For several years Gertie Jones provided the teas, which consisted of sandwiches and home-made cakes. Gertie would load all the food, and other necessary items, into her father's trap and drive off at a steady trot, with Bonny the horse between the shafts. In later years, when Gertie's sisters, Ivy and Mrs Margetts, made the teas with Mrs Petrie, a perambulator was used as the means of transportation.

An old newspaper cutting, loaned by Miss Josephine Shirley (Gertie's daughter), records the annual meeting of the cricket club held on Friday 9 February 1923.

The President was the Rt. Hon. Lord Sherborne, Mr R.F. Stratton was elected Chairman. The Secretary presented the Balance Sheet showing a credit balance of £3 4s. 1d. The Balance Sheet was passed subject to audit, and a hearty vote of thanks was proposed from the chair to the Treasurer and Secretary for so successful a financial year. During the Season of 1922, the Club played 18 matches; winning 10, losing 4 and drawing 4.

Officers elected were:

President – Rt. Hon. Lord Sherborne.

Vice-Presidents – The Hon. Lady Sherborne,
                Mrs R. Gray, Mr R. Gray,
                Mr R.F. Stratton, Mr W. Tremaine
                Revd G. Warner, Mr A. Lockhart,
                Mr G. Freeman, Mr A. Handy.

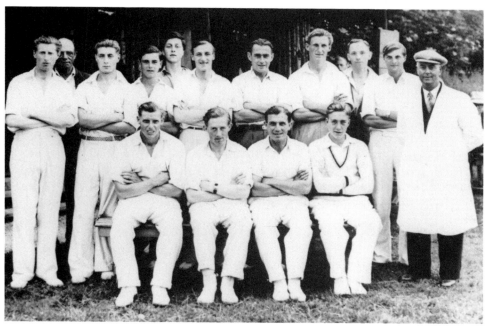

Sherborne cricket team in ?. Back row, left to right: D. Saunders, Mr Rigsby, B. Saunders, A. Hickman, P. Mayes, J. Ashworth, Henry Shepherd, R. Hayward, Mr Herrin, I. Waterston, Mr Hemmings. Seated: P. Ash, E. Saunders, H. Taylor, J. Stevens.

Treasurer – Mr R. Gray.
Secretary – Mr H. Demer.
Captain – Mr H. Demer.
Vice-Captain – Mr A. Tye.
The General Committee comprised: the Captain, the secretary, R.W. Houlton, E. Mumford, R. Saunders, C. Large, E. Hopkins, J.O. Lloyd, F. Taylor and E. Tyres.
Selection Committee: The Captain, Vice Captain, R.W. Houlton and E. Mumford.
It was decided that Subscriptions for the coming season should be set at: Adults over 16 years 2s. 6d.
Under 16 years 1s. 0d.
The Secretary expressed the idea that it would prove possible to form a second XI for the coming season, and it was agreed that a further meeting should be called, on Friday April 13th. Last date for subscriptions was March 3rd.
The club expressed their gratitude to Miss G. Jones, for undertaking to supply teas, and they decided to join with the Football Club in presenting Miss Jones with a present. Mrs W. Johnson was asked to undertake refreshments for the coming season.
The meeting closed with a hearty vote of thanks to the Chairman, Mr R.F. Stratton.

A whist drive, held the next evening, was also reported in the newspaper as follows:

> A very successful Whist Drive, in aid of the Football Club, was held in the
> Reading Room on Saturday, Feby. 10th: Winners were:
> Ladies: 1st prize – Mrs R. Renn
>   2nd prize – Miss G. Jones
>   consolation prize – Nurse Hambling
> Gentlemen: 1st prize – Mr Weaver
>   2nd prize – Mr J. Williams.
> At the conclusion Mr E. Mumford, on behalf of the Cricket and Football
> teams, presented Miss G. Jones with a mahogany clock, subscribed for by the
> members on the occasion of her forthcoming marriage. Miss Jones replied
> suitably, returning thanks for this handsome present.

A third social event was held a few days later, as reported in the *East Cotswold
Church Monthly*:

> The Women's Institute held their fifth Birthday Party on Tuesday Feb. 13th,
> 1923. After an excellent tea, including an iced birthday cake, a Whist Drive
> was held from 7.30 to 11 p.m., open to all members, husbands and friends.
> The prize winners were as follows:
> Ladies: 1st prize – Miss Ivy Jones (a silver and enamel fruit
> basket) presented by Mrs Corbett.
>   2nd prize – Mrs A. O'Reilly (1 lb of jumper wool).
> Gentlemen: 1st prize – Mr B. Williams (cigarette lighter).
>   2nd prize – Mr C. Jones (50 cigarettes).
> A presentation, which took the form of a dinner cruet, was made to Miss G.
> Jones on Saturday Feby. 10th by Lady Sherborne, on behalf of members of
> the WI as a mark of appreciation and esteem on the occasion of her marriage.

The birthday party was held in the Reading Room, but the president, Lady
Sherborne, was unfortunately unable to attend. Mrs R. Gray was a welcome guest,
as was the vicar, the Revd G. Warner. The report goes on to say:

> The Hon. Secretary, Mrs Dow, must feel very proud in celebrating their 5th
> Birthday in such a happy, social way which attained a record attendance of
> members and well-wishers, now men, where is your Institute?

A few years later the Women's Institute ceased to function in Sherborne, but on
Monday 24 November 1947 Mrs Herrin called a formation meeting to explore the
possibility of its revival. The meetings was well attended, and of the thirty-four
people present thirty-one put their names forward for nomination to the committee. At the first monthly meeting, held on 1 December 1947, Mrs Warner, a
VCO, was in the chair and Mrs Wallington, with Mrs Joynes, from Great
Rissington WI, were appointed as tellers.

The ballot for the committee resulted in the following members being elected:

President –   The Hon. Mrs Joan Dutton (later to become
                     Lady Sherborne)
Vice-President –   Mrs B.A. Demer
Secretary –   Mrs M.G. Herrin
Treasurer –   Mrs D.K. Russell
Members –   Mrs C. Harris, Mrs W. Johnson
                     Mrs M. Larner, Mrs H. Robinson
                     Mrs D. Stevens, Mrs I. Tremaine

The annual subscription was set at 2s. 6d. The age of seventeen years was set as the minimum for admittance to membership. Owing to the new-found interest in the WI it proved practical to appoint four different members each month to be responsible for the provision of refreshments. It was agreed that a charge of 1d. should be made for a cup of tea, the same charge for a sandwich or biscuit, and also for a programme (the penny going towards the printing costs).

It was also agreed to compile a rota of members responsible for the social half hour each month. The first of these featured Mrs Hill and Mrs Vera Hayward performing a sketch entitled 'The Umbrella Ladies'. The first competition, 'How many items can you get in a matchbox', was won by Mrs Hill with 132.

The Institute was attached to the Cotswold Group and arrangements were made for members to attend their first group meeting, held at Chedworth on 26 November 1948. These annual meetings were always well attended, with members working keenly together to exhibit in the competition, although it has to be reported that on occasion the judges' decision regarding the outcome did not always meet with unanimous approval.

Over the years a wide variety of talks, exhibitions, demonstrations, film shows etc. have taken place and have been much enjoyed by those present.

Dressmaking classes were arranged, however the overall results proved a little disappointing, with the only exception being the lampshade making. Basket weaving, under the expert instruction of the Revd H. Cheales of Wyck Rissington (who frequently arrived fresh from attending and milking his cows), resulted in a varied selection of useful baskets. The most successful class was that of upholstery, where members stripped chairs and stools, and renovated them beyond recognition, and all involved were extremely proud of their achievements.

The WI was very much indebted to Mr Herrin at that time, for providing storage room for the pieces of furniture, springs, stuffing and the multifarious tools required for the project.

For many years the highlight of the WI year was the annual party, when each member could bring along a friend, male or female. Mouth-watering refreshments were provided by the members. The programme for the party of 1950 consisted of games and dancing, a talk by Mr Bramwell Hill, 'Appointment with Cheer', the birthday cake was made by Mrs E. Cambray and Mrs Ballard, and music was provided by Mr Barnett of Brockworth.

For several years, a garden meeting was held at Stones Farm, by kind permission of Mrs W. Limbrick, who always provided dishes of fresh strawberries, or

Members and guest at a W.I. party in the 1950s. Left to right: Mrs Maunders, Mrs Newport, Mrs Tremaine, Mrs Moody, Mrs Thomas and Ron Hayward.

raspberries and cream. On one amusing and memorable occasion, following a lively dance on the damp lawn, there appeared a very large number of worms!

On 21 October 1956, forty WI members attended a dinner in the school to mark the 100th monthly meeting since the group was reformed. After an excellent meal (prepared by members) and entertainment by Mrs E. Margetts, with a song, and Mrs H. Tufnell, who told a ghost story, there followed community singing led by Mrs Connie Leach, with Mrs I. Tremaine at the piano.

On 17 November 1987, members celebrated their fortieth birthday party in the school. The three remaining founder members, Mrs Herrin, Mrs Mayes and Mrs Longhurst, cut the birthday cake made by Mrs Mavis Taylor. The President, Mrs Hilda Ellis, presented the three 'originals' with miniature red rose trees to mark the occasion. Entertainment was provided by Mr Martin Dee who spoke on how to blow a hunting horn, followed by making music from 'any old iron'.

The widely held belief that the WI is all 'jam and Jerusalem' is far from the truth, for members pursue a variety of interests. A tennis tournament has been running for many years, indeed on one occasion Mavis Taylor, partnered by Julie Young, won the County Cup at Lillishaw and were runners up in the final held at Queens Club. Mrs Christine Taylor and her partner were runners up in the county badminton final.

A friendly rounders match against Northleach was much enjoyed despite the result (Northleach were definite winners). This was followed by a lovely supper at The Sherborne Arms.

Members did not disgrace themselves in the many skittles matches and on several occasions a member has attended the finals of the county scrabble competition at Gloucester. The quiz team came a very commendable second one year at the county quiz final. For the winter of 1991 the county is organizing its first darts competition and there is little doubt that the Sherborne ladies will be 'raring to go' for that elusive '180'!

The WI still thrives since its revival forty-two years ago, even though membership now includes ladies from the Barringtons and Windrush, and several incumbents have moved to Bourton-on-the-Water.

The Mother's Union was also a thriving club which started when the former WI ceased to be. The Hon. Mrs Charles Dutton (Lord Sherborne's mother) started the meetings at her house ('The Cottage' now renamed 'Brook House'), and following her death, Mrs Isobel Tremaine succeeded to the leadership and held the meetings in her home at Sherborne Farm. The meetings usually started with prayers and a hymn, and following this the members busied themselves with sewing or knitting. Excellent patchwork and embroidered bedspreads were made and subsequently raffled for church funds. It was a 'red letter day' in 1955, when the Sherborne branch, after working extremely hard, received their Mother's Union banner. A service for the blessing of the banner was held in the church. Gertie Renn attended by Cis Hayward and Elizabeth Johnson, three of the longest-serving members, had the honour of carrying the banner for the service.

In the ensuing years, the banner was carried on many occasions at Mother's Union festivals in Gloucester cathedral, Cirencester parish church and Northleach

'The Cottage', photographed here in 1877 and recently renamed Brook House, was home of The Hon. Mrs C. Dutton, mother of James, Lord Sherborne.

church. Isobel Tremaine proved to be a diligent leader and members responded to her dedication by applying themselves, to the best of their abilities, to any allotted task. Many interesting outings were organized and enjoyed, with the following being just a few; Windsor Castle, Blenheim Palace, Worcester Porcelain Factory, Salisbury Cathedral and Berkeley Castle.

Marjorie Mayes became the leader upon the death of Isobel Tremaine, but numbers diminished for many reasons, old age and infirmity to name but two. The Union, also losing popularity with the younger generation who saw it as an 'older woman's organization', finally came to an end in the late 1970s.

Guy Fawkes Night was an annual event which was looked forward to with eager anticipation by the village children. Due to the village being divided naturally into halves, there were always two bonfires; one at the Top End, on a piece of wasteland down Ash Hole and another at the Bottom End in a field opposite cottages Nos 45 and 46.

For weeks prior to the event the village lads collected all available combustible material and transported it to their respective sites with the aid of the Scouts' truck, loaned by the Sherborne estate. This truck was normally used by the painters to move their paints and ladders.

Until the outbreak of the Second World War, the Reading Room was open every evening for the men to meet and play darts, draughts, cards or dominoes etc. A successful darts team won the Farmington and District Darts League Cup in 1937. The Reading Room was also used for chapel meetings on Sunday evenings, with the preachers usually coming from Bourton-on-the-Water or other local villages.

On one occasion when Mr Collett was the attendant preacher, and had left his pony and trap tied to the gate, the young village lads decided to play a prank on him. Just prior to the conclusion of the service they led the pony through the gate, closed it, then pushed the shafts of the trap through the gate bars and re-harnessed the pony. When Mr Collett emerged he surveyed the scene with some bewilderment, much to the amusement of the perpetrators who then put everything to rights, to allow his journey home. Another trick played by the youngsters was 'tick and spider' on the cottage window panes, using pins and buttons, and a long piece of strong thread. Knocking on adjacent cottage doors, having first tied the doorknobs together with string, and watching the neighbours trying to open their doors, with lighted candle in hand, was the source of much merriment.

During the Second World War the Reading Room was the venue for all of the village social events, despite having no public toilets. It was the only suitable building that could be blacked out successfully.

Weekly whist drives were held to raise funds for the returning servicemen and women. Harold Robinson was the treasurer of the 'Coming Home Fund'. It was fortunate for them that Mr and Mrs Robinson decided to come to the village one weekend, at the height of the blitz, to get some relief from the bombing, as their home area received a direct hit and everyone in the air-raid shelter lost their lives.

Socials, held on Saturday evenings, were attended by the military personnel occupying Sherborne House and an attempt was made to dance on the flagstone floor. The popular dances at that time were the barn dance, the military two step, hands, knees and bumps-a-daisy, the conga, the Lambeth walk and the palais glide.

Games such as 'kissing on the mat' when the music ceased, 'pass the parcel', 'musical chairs' and many others were entered into with great gusto and enjoyed by one and all. Music was provided by Gerald Rachael and Freddie Turner playing their piano accordions. Cookery classes and demonstrations took place in the afternoons, for a short while, to show how to make best use of the meagre food rations, including the very versatile powdered egg.

During the war years there was a health and beauty class, run by Miss Lettie Morrison who lodged at the Dairy Farm with Mr and Mrs Lane, while working at the Maintenance Unit at RAF Little Rissington.

The class was held on the lawn at Dairy Farm, weather permitting, and on more inclement days it was held in the school. As with modern aerobics, movements were performed to music supplied by a record player. During the summer months the girls gave displays at the village fetes. On one occasion, when the fete was held at The Cottage, a steep bank had to be negotiated by the girls when making their entrance. Bare foot, wearing long, flowing dresses, with arms outstretched and holding panels of flimsy material as wings, a spectator was heard to say that the young ladies resembled a group of fairies making an entrance (some fairies, since some of the members taking part were very well built!).

Those partaking in the health and beauty class were as follows (maiden names): Sheila Tremaine, Mary Hayward, Eileen Larner, Myrtle Larner, Sybil Margetts, Evelyn Saunders, Eunice Hooper, Betty Saunders, Sybil Dodson, Lettie Morrison (teacher), Doreen Paxford, Dorothy Reeves and Violet Oliver.

Before the war, Sunday was looked upon as being a day of rest and for attending church or chapel, after which the family would gather in the parents' home for tea.

Health and beauty class, 1943. Back row, left to right: S. Tremaine, M. Hayward, E. Larner, M. Larner, S. Margetts, E. Saunders, Eyra Saunders, E. Hooper. Front row: Betty Saunders, Elsie Saunders, S. Dodson, L. Morrison (teacher), D. Paxford, D. Reeves, V. Oliver.

Knitting and sewing were frowned upon, as were the washing and ironing of clothes. The men performed just the basic essentials in the garden, gathering fruit and vegetables for the midday meal.

Whole families were to be seen enjoying walks together in the summer evenings, picking wild flowers, searching for birds' nests, and the children loved to take note of the registration numbers of the few vehicles that travelled the A40.

The summer and autumn months were busy ones, gathering blackberries and crab apples from the hedgerows for making jams and jellies. Eggs, when plentiful, were preserved in waterglass and stored in earthenware crocks. Runner beans were packed into earthenware jars, with alternate layers of salt, to preserve them for winter use when other vegetables were in short supply.

Larder shelves would be stocked with jams, jellies, chutneys, various pickles including onions, beetroot, walnuts and red cabbage etc., as well as wines of all descriptions; blackberry, cowslip, rhubarb, parsnip, damson, ginger, elderberry, orange and raspberry vinegar. Many of the families brewed their own malt and hops beer.

After the war ended, life in the village totally changed, with the returning servicemen and women, together with redundant war workers, finding employment difficult to obtain despite the promises made to them that their jobs awaited.

Lord and Lady Sherborne were now resident in Windrush Manor, leaving Sherborne House empty, household staff were no longer required and the estate could not afford to employ the same number of workers as before. With the changes in agriculture and the advent of machinery, farm workers were not required in such great numbers either. Consequently, the younger people started to move away, some to the homes of their spouses, met during the war, others to towns and cities to find work, or to retrain for a different occupation. Having travelled extensively and experienced better living conditions, they were determined to strive for a better lifestyle.

This state of affairs had a detrimental effect on the social life of the village, coupled with the fact that over the ensuing years families became smaller. Both cricket and football teams, having flourished for so long, felt the effect of the declining numbers of young people. First to fall was the cricket team and within the last few years the football team has also ceased to exist.

The Reading Room was no longer the nightly meeting place for the men, but it was still in use as the school canteen and occasionally for social events.

A Christmas party, held for the school children, was organized by a committee of village ladies for several years. Vera Hayward was secretary and Alice Tufnell was treasurer. Other helpers were Mrs E. Cambray, Mrs D. Stevens, Mrs D. Lester, Mrs P. Mills, Mrs M. Hanks, Mrs P. Sallis and Mrs C. Hayward. Collections and prize bingos were arranged to raise funds. Two members would spend a day in Gloucester selecting and purchasing presents. A Christmas tree was supplied by the estate and for many years Annie Limbrick very much enjoyed playing the role of Father Christmas. By 1970, the Reading Room had been turned into a Sports and Social Club, under the chairmanship of Cynthia Margetts, with a committee of ten or eleven. Within the first five years business was flourishing. This allowed extensive structural alterations to be carried out, including the incorporation of the

The winning Darts Team in 1937. Back row, left to right: Teddy Margetts, Tom Saunders, Lionel Cambray, Stuart Saunders, Ray Mathews. Front row: Greg Morse, Jim Smith, Teddy Williams, Steve Williams.

neighbouring property, No. 44. A new bar was erected, a lounge room fitted out, and a cellar room and spacious car park provided.

A happy social life was established with well-attended harvest suppers, Christmas dinners and social evenings. Annual fêtes were still being held, and one year there was a carnival which included a pram push, starting at Top End and finishing at the club, with several watering stops on the way, where the pusher had to consume a pint of beer. Paul Mustoe and partner won the event. The carnival was headed by the Social Club Queen, the first being Marlene Long, attended by Hilary Mustoe and Rosemary Clark who were chosen at a previous social evening.

To mark the occasion of Queen Elizabeth II's Silver Jubilee, a weeping silver birch tree was planted in the garden of the Social Club, and a box, containing a photograph of the committee members, a price list and several other items relevant to that time, was buried beside the tree.

Darts has always been the main sporting activity of the club, but it is now shared with pool and a clay pigeon shoot. Paul Saunders succeeded Cynthia Margetts as chairman in 1983.

In the early 1960s some of the cottages were offered for sale to the sitting tenants, and over the last two decades more have been sold off, as they became empty, at prices far beyond the reach of the young village couples. In common with many old villages this has resulted in an influx of outside people, and meant the loss of the close-knit community and traditional lifestyle, remembered by the few original residents of the village.

CHAPTER TEN

Personalities

James Bradley is undoubtedly Sherborne's most famous son. His parents hailed from County Durham, moving via Hampnett to Sherborne where his father worked as steward on the estate. James was born in Sherborne in March 1693, the third son to Jane Pound, who was from a wealthy Wiltshire family. His uncle, the Revd James Pound, earned a healthy living in Wanstead which paid for James's education while at Northleach Grammar School, and also for his upkeep at Balliol College, Oxford. When Northleach Grammar School was re-established in 1925, one of the three houses was named 'Bradley' in his honour.

James took holy orders and became a curate at Hereford where his duties included being secretary to the Bishop of Hereford. From 1719 to 1721 he augmented his living by taking a parish in Carmarthen. Due to the endeavours of his uncle James Pound, in 1721 James was offered the post of Savilian Professor of Astrology at Oxford. He married a daughter of Samuel Peach of Chalford. In 1729 he became a leader in experimental philosophy at Oxford. While in this post two of his oustanding achievements were the discovery of the aberration of light and the mutation of the earth's axis. Upon the death of his great friend, Edmond Halley, James was appointed to the position of Astronomer Royal.

King George II granted him a pension of £250 a year in addition to his salary. 'In consideration of his great skill and knowledge in several branches of astronomy and other parts of mathematics which have proved so useful to the trade and navigation of the Kingdom.'

James died in 1762 at the age of sixty-nine and was buried in the churchyard at Minchinhampton, where there is an inscription to his memory on a brass plate fixed to his tomb.

Mrs Hannah Tate, born 10 April 1809 and died 23 November 1910, is believed to hold the record for longevity in the village at 101 years. Her husband was the village tailor whose workroom was a building situated to the rear of No. 52 Sherborne (as recorded in *Kelly's Directory* of 1876).

Mr Tom Matthews brought his family to Sherborne in 1904 and moved into No. 52, while Mrs Tate was still in residence. Mrs Margaret Mate, the only surviving member of the Matthews family, cannot recall any agreement as to this situation, but she does recall her mother nursing Mrs Tate towards the end of her days. A room in the house was always referred to as 'Mrs Tate's room'.

Tom Matthews brought his large family to Sherborne in order to join the staff as foreman painter and decorator on the estate and became very well known and respected. He was secretary of the Sherborne and Windrush Pig Club, Branch

Mrs H. Tate (1809–1910), Sherborne's oldest known inhabitant to date.

Secretary of the Cirencester Friendly Society and a member of the local unemployment council which met in Northleach and later in Cheltenham. In 1918 he was appointed a justice of the peace for Gloucestershire and sat on the Northleach Bench. He was appointed a governor of Westwood's Grammar School, a member of the Northleach RDC, Vice-Chairman of the Sherborne Parish Council and a manager of the village school. Tom's interest in politics followed the Liberal movement, and as a direct result of being appointed local agent for the Liberal party, he was dismissed from his employment on the estate (such was the power of the Lords of the Manor in those days). He was, however, allowed to remain in his cottage so long as he paid an annual rent to the estate in 1936 of £6 4s. 0d. for the 'permitted number' of 10½ persons at No. 52.

Having been trained as a signwriter in his youth, he was able to earn his living engraving coffin plates and writing signs. He wrote the Sherborne column in the weekly village news section of the *Wilts and Glos Standard*, giving details of births, funerals, weddings, WI meetings, in addition to sports and social events. He was always willing to oblige with his advice on any important letters that required writing by a villager, or even taking the job in hand himself.

His sporting interests were cricket and football, where he was sadly missed when forced to leave the village through ill health. He finally died at the age of eighty-seven.

William H. Limbrick took over the tenancy at Stones Farm in 1947, having come from Chitterne in Wiltshire, via Ley Mary Farm in Windrush. His younger days were spent with his wife, Annie, farming in Canada, whence he acquired a slight North American accent. Within two years of arriving at Stones Farm he took over the tenancy of Home Farm from Mr Bertie Blake whose mother retained occupancy of the farmhouse. Upon the death of old Mrs Blake, William's son Thomas, along with his wife Peggy and children, Jean, Bill and Roy, moved from Chitterne to take up residence.

William and Thomas carried on mixed farming, running a milking herd of Fresians and for a short time a pedigree herd of Jersey cows at Stones Farm, they reared calves for beef, ran a flock of sheep, reared pigs and specialized in Broad White Breasted turkeys, managed by Lionel Preston, on Home Farm. Mixed cereals were grown as well as seeds for seed production. In 1949 the cereal crop comprised:

Pioneer Winter Barley;
Abed Kenia and Earl Barley (a recent introduction by Dr Hunter, which was put on the market in 1946 by the NIAB);
Jubilee Gem Wheat, grown for its short, stiff straw.

The oats were a pedigree strain of S.225. Thirty-two acres were planted with:

S.143 Cocksfoot;
S.100 White Clover;
S.23 Ryegrass;
S.48 Timothy;
S.215 Meadow Fescue; and a Cotswold strain of Broad Red Clover.

The barley, grown for malting, was sold directly to the Cheltenham and Hereford Brewery. A few acres of potatoes were also grown for seed crop. W.H. Limbrick and Son were the first farmers in the village to own a self-propelled combine harvester. Delivered in package form it was assembled on the farm by the agricultural engineers from whom it was bought. They also owned a corn drier and cleaner which initially operated at Catts Abbey before being moved to Windrush Camp some years later.

By 1954 the Limbricks had added the acreage of Manor Farm at Windrush to their tenancy and they had purchased Bourton Hill Farm. At this point in time the workforce comprised thirty-four full- and part-time employees, eleven of which were females. Tragedy, in the form of foot and mouth disease, struck on 8 January 1957, among the pigs on Home Farm. All the livestock had to be slaughtered and buried in lime pits, excavated expressly for the purpose, in Folly Field near the A40. The surrounding area was limed out and fenced off from use for several years. All the Home Farm buildings were fumigated and lime washed, and all farms in the area had disinfecting sites at their entrances for some considerable time. A long period elapsed before Home Farm could again be stocked with animals. It was thought at the time that starlings which frequented the pigsties had brought the disease. Pigs were never again to be reared on Home Farm.

In 1959 William Limbrick was awarded the OBE for services to agriculture. He was a Committee Member of the Three Counties Show, Chairman of the Moreton-in-Marsh Agricultural Show and Chairman of the Northleach RDC, where he campaigned to get mains electricity connected to the village. He realized this ambition when his farmhouse was the first to be connected in November 1948. He was also among the first in the village to own a television set. Another of his goals while Chairman of the Northleach RDC was to get mains water and sewerage installed. Unfortunately he did not live to see the latter ambition fulfilled. William died peacefully in his chair at the height of the turkey-plucking season in December 1964, at the age of eighty-two.

Mr Hopkins, a keen cricketer and demon fast bowler, replaced Robert Gray as estate agent in the late 1920s. From this time to the mid-1930s the estate was run by the Country Gentlemens' Association. Mr Lidden, their representative, would visit Sherborne periodically, travelling down from London to do so.

Mervyn Mullett was the estate clerk in the late 1920s and another good cricketer. Mervyn's father, Lord Sherborne's coachman, was nicknamed 'Punch', due to his large nose and protruding chin. Mrs Mullett, who was a short, plump woman, became the talking point of the village through falling out of her bedroom window while in the process of cleaning it. Her only injuries, apart from a sorely dented pride, were a few bruises!

Mr Flower, a member of the Flowers brewery family, replaced Mr Hopkins as agent. He much preferred visiting the farm tenants to sitting behind an office desk. His favourite saying when aroused or annoyed was 'Ye Gods and little fishes'.

Walter Tufnell took over the task of estate clerk from Mervyn Mullett in 1936, and was joined by **Wilfred Mayes** in the position of estate agent in 1937.

W.H. Limbrick & Sons employees in 1954. Back row, left to right: V. Strange, H. Bunting, A. Barber, E. Strange, W. Harding, W. Thornton, W. Strange, M. Wilsdon. Centre row: L. Thompson, J. Harding, Mrs Strange (holding John Harding), J. Higgs, E. Margetts, J. Smith, W. Radband, C. Vincent, D. Margetts, L. Preston, H. Hooper, R. Harding, C. Harding, A. Wright, M. Hayley, A. Hawkes-Reed. Seated: M. Vincent, W. Ind, C. Margetts, S.

Longhurst, Mrs A. Limbrick, Mr W. Limbrick, Mr T. Limbrick, Mrs P. Limbrick and Roy, S. Boucher, E. Hooper, M. Wilsdon. Employed at the time but missing from the photograph: M. Haviland, D. Mills and G. Swinford.

Prior to the outbreak of the Second World War, the estate workers would collect their wages from the office, while the workers in Sherborne House had their wages delivered by the clerk. The butler, who enjoyed a flutter on the horses, was responsible for distributing the wages to the men. The cook/housekeeper, a plump and jolly lady who had to use a large earphone as she was hard of hearing, would hand out the women's wages.

Because he had no radio, **George Rainbow**, foreman of the labourers (hedgers and ditchers), used the newspapers as his sole source of information and reading was not one of his strong points. One day when he was collecting his wages, just before the outbreak of the war, he said to the clerk, 'What do you think of them Creshies?'

'What Creshies, George?', came the reply.

'They Creshies that be 'avin' a go at that 'itler bloke.'

'I see.'

'I allus did think there'd be trouble between 'itler and they Creshies. They be goin' to start up another war thee'st know.'

'Oh, I don't know.'

'Well I be tellin' thee they will, thee'st mind my words and see if'n I b'aint right.'

With this, George turned and walked away with a knowing smile on his face as if to say, 'Now I've given him something to think about.' It was later discovered that the 'Creshies' George alluded to were in fact the Czechs.

Thomas Dow, the head forester in the 1930s, was a dour Scotsman who had a great regard for the well-being of his woodsmen.

Arthur Mitchell, the head gardener, had to be constantly on his toes as Lady Ethel Sherborne took a keen interest in the garden and had a propensity for turning up at any hour of the day to browse among the shrubberies.

Alan Hill, the head gamekeeper, was a man of Norfolk origin who immersed himself in village affairs. In addition to being Chairman of the Parish Council for many years, he was also Chairman of the Pig Club, Chairman of the Reading Room Committee and a great enthusiast of village whist drives. On shooting days he controlled his guns, keepers and beaters by blowing different notes on his bugle.

Charlie Lane, who lived at the Dairy Farm, was herdsman of Lord Sherborne's Pedigree Jersey cows. Charlie took the records of the herd to the estate office each week and frequently among his notes would appear 'calf borned today'. **Mrs Lane** was a very pleasant, large lady who made excellent, but very strong wine. One Christmas Eve the clerk called to wish them both a 'Merry Christmas', and after sampling Mrs Lane's cheer, he mounted his bicycle to return home, but only succeeded in reaching the roadside before falling off.

Thomas Shepherd, the odd-job man at Sherborne House, was employed to keep the bunkers full of sawn logs and to attend two stoke holes. He was a regular spectator at village football games and had a memory good enough to give detailed reports of games long past.

Ernest Walker, Tom's neighbour, was a man who quarrelled with no one. One of

Mr Alan Hill, head gamekeeper on the estate, 1920–1930s.

the finest stonewallers in the district, Ernest would quarry the stone at Cat's Abbey to ensure that the Park walls were kept in fine order. Ernest was never heard to use a swearword, instead he would exclaim 'I jolly well do' or 'I jolly well am'.

Lewis Lord, one of the underkeepers, lived at Northfield. During partridge shooting, when approaching a field of mustard he would instruct the beaters, ''ere thee b'st blokes, get into that yeller tack'.

During a visit of fellow underkeeper **Bill Spinks** and wife, who lived at Allen's Lodge (long since demolished), and following a cup of tea and a snack, Lew's wife suggested that he might tap the barrel of wine he had made the previous year. Lew ambled to the larder and turned on the tap, and when nothing flowed he removed the bung and found the barrel totally devoid of 'cheer'. 'Where's it gone to?' asked Mrs Lord. Looking extremely bashful, Lew solved the mystery by confessing that whenever he had felt the urge he inserted a straw through the bung hole and had taken a couple of sips. The disappointed visitors had to settle for another cup of tea!

Andy O'Reilly, Alf Mills and **Jim Larner** were the painters and decorators. Jim, a chain smoker of Woodbine cigarettes, had a moustache stained quite ginger through smoking each cigarette to the last puff. He was an avid gardener who grew beautiful double, dark blue, Parma violets under cold frames. His wife and daughter would sell them for 6d. a bunch in one of the shops on the Promenade in Cheltenham.

Alec Cook, who lived in Windrush, worked in the gardens for many years. He had to walk to work six days a week and kept such regular time that one could set one's watch by him. His favourite saying was 'If's so be'.

Teddy Williams, who was employed by the County Council in the 1950s to keep the village tidy, was a swarthy-complexioned man with a mop of black hair. He loved greyhound racing and would spend almost every weekend at the track in Gloucester. He kept the village street in tip-top condition, weed free and tidy. (We need another Teddy Williams in the village today.)

Mrs Maria Newport is still remembered as one of the real characters of the village. She was a very jovial lady who always had a smile on her face and was the life and soul of social gatherings. Her favourite 'party trick' was singing 'My Old Man' and 'There's a Hole in my Bucket', which she would perform with Mrs Maunders. Maria's husband, Frank, who was the village taxi driver for many years.

Sid Morse, was a general farm worker for Mr Tremaine, who, surprisingly, quite enjoyed cleaning out drains. One day while feeding his pigs one escaped into the village street. Sid was short in stature and slightly bow legged and in the confusion of trying to get the offending animal back into its sty it suddenly ran between his legs, unbalancing him, and to everyone's amusement careered off down the street with Sidney astride, facing backwards.

Billy Larner's tale was of the day he sold some potatoes to a fellow workman, charging him half a crown, which was never paid. Billy was heard to say, 'If I'd known he wasn't going to pay, I'd've charged him five bob'.

Billy was a good stonemason who, tragically, lost his life in 1943 when a wall he was demolishing collapsed on top of him.

Charlie Jones came to Sherborne, from Windrush, in 1907. He arrived with his family of ten to take over the village shop, at No. 48, from Mrs Sally Stevens who was no longer capable of running it, due to her predilection for home brew. As a haulier, when not carrying for the estate, Charlie brought coal from Bourton-on-the-Water railway station and sold it around the village for 1s. (5p) per hundredweight. He was a short, robust, red-faced, bewhiskered man who loved children; in his later years he could be found standing at his gate when the children passed to and from school greeting them with, 'Hello my little maids and chappies'. His great love was to visit the local markets, Cheltenham Thursday market being one of his regular stops. Charlie's obituary read:

> The villagers of Sherborne heard with deep regret that Charlie Jones passed away on Monday night. His death in his 92nd year, removes a well loved and familiar figure. He always had a smile and a few words for his friends and neighbours. Though not a native of Sherborne, he had lived in the village for

40 years, and his stories of country life, from when he started work as a ploughboy at the age of 8 years, were listened to with great interest. Farewell to a Grand Old Gentleman'.

Clem Jones, the eldest son to Charlie, carried on the haulage business when his father retired. For many years he assisted with the sheep and lambing at Home Farm. He slaughtered the animals required for the table of the Big House, but was always rather reluctant to kill the spring lamb for the Easter Sunday table, knowing that it had not had much of a taste of life. For miles around, Clem was the man called on to kill pigs for cottagers' own home consumption. This he would achieve by sticking them, then burning off the body hairs on a straw fire. Another of Clem's tasks, before the GCC took over, was to collect the ashes from the village cottages. He also supplied the horse power required to pull the tar barrel when the A40, from the Oxford/Gloucestershire boundary to Andoversford, and the local village streets were first surfaced with tarmac. Ern Souls aided him in this task, along with the County Council labourers.

A regular topic of Clem's conversation was of the time he helped haul the stone used to build the West Lodges in 1911. It has been rumoured that this stone was obtained by removing the top two layers of the Park wall, originally built 9 feet high to confine the estate deer, but research has failed to confirm this.

Clem, an accomplished bell-ringer, was a member of the church bell ringers and hand-bell ringers. He was also the last person to utilize the common land, where he grazed his horses.

Fred Saunders lived most of his life at No. 1 Sherborne which had been the home of wheelwrights for 170 years (see page 160). In 1921 young Fred was taken on as an apprentice wheelwright by **William Scregg**. There he worked until William's death at the age of eighty-one, when he took over the business.

At one time William Scregg employed as many as eight men and boys making and repairing farm carts and wagons. Timber, which they felled themselves, was purchased from Sherborne estate. The wood was sawn and then left, for three years, in the yard to season. Oak was used for the wheel spokes, elm for the hubs and felloes (wheel rims) and ash for the cart shafts. The iron rims were shaped from flat bars. As many as ten at a time were heated in a huge wood fire. When red hot, they were slipped over the wheels and then rapidly cooled with water; this process would cause them to shrink on to the wheels, pulling the wood tight and thereby making the complete unit tremendously strong. Similar small rims were bonded either side of the hub to prevent splitting. The largest wheels made were 5 feet 6 inches in diameter with up to sixteen spokes.

The yard also made wagons and carts. Fred estimated that up to the Second World War they had made some fifty or sixty carts (two-wheeled vehicles), trolleys (flat, four-wheeled wagons) and jumpers (four-wheeled vehicles with low sides), as well as innumerable wooden 'drags' (horse-drawn bars fitted with iron spikes for breaking up the soil). Just prior to the War Fred started to fit the wagons with modern wheels and pneumatic tyres, but when the rubber became scarce due to war requirements he returned to the old methods.

Fred was not required for military service, as the Ministry of Agriculture felt that he was better employed keeping the agricultural machinery in good working order for food production. He also repaired elevators and threshing machines among other tasks. In 1935 it took Fred ten days to make a cart for sale at £14. The last two wagons he made, just before the outbreak of the Second World War, were for a Taynton farmer. His initial price was £50 for the two, but he was eventually knocked down to £45. From 1935 until 1947 Fred doubled as the village undertaker. His last funeral was that of Eleanor Hill, wife of Alan Hill the gamekeeper. The bearers were Frank Newport, Tom Shepherd, Bill Hayward and Will Johnson. The brass coffin plate was inscribed by Tom Matthews.

With the inception of mass production of farm equipment, Fred, ably assisted by his youngest son Graham, took to repairing gates, planting trees and repairing fencing on the Sherborne estate and in the surrounding villages. He was also called upon to destroy wasps' nests and rat infestations. Approximately sixty years ago Fred helped to make the panelled and wrought-iron gates at the entrance to Farmington estate, and they are still in existence today. There are very few Cotswold carts remaining today, Fred's skills are a thing of the past.

Basil Howse was born in Aldsworth and lived there all his life, but any record of past life in Sherborne would not be complete without mentioning Basil, whose bus service played such an important part in the lives of the villagers. Basil's forefathers once owned Winson Manor, but it was his father who started a carrier service to Cirencester using a horse and carriage. Basil graduated from the horse-drawn vehicle to his first bus which had a canvas top and sides, and seats down the side, and was entered by steps from the rear. The service into Cheltenham through the villages of Aldsworth, the Barringtons, Windrush, Sherborne and Northleach started in the early 1930s. This service scheduled the bus to leave Sherborne at 1.30 p.m. on Tuesday, Thursday, Friday and Saturday, as well as 11 a.m. Thursday and 4 p.m. Saturday. The return trip departed Cheltenham at approximately 5.30 p.m. and on Saturdays at 10.30 p.m.

Basil also ran a service through to Cirencester on Wednesdays and Fridays. It started at Burford on Wednesday, but on Friday it ran through the villages starting at Aldsworth, through Sherborne, Windrush, the Barringtons and Taynton to Burford, where he stayed for two hours. The return journey went back through the villages and then on to Cirencester for a couple of hours' shopping. The bus then went back to Burford and left once again for Cirencester at 5.00 p.m. in order to catch the evening show at the cinema. There was also a cinema run to Cirencester on Sunday evenings.

The fare to Cirencester in 1952 was 2s. return, and the Cheltenham run was 2s. 6d. return. The bus to Cheltenham now costs 75p each way.

Basil often spoke of the day when, with his brother Jack (who was a carpenter on Sherborne estate), he carried a portable organ from Sherborne to Aldsworth on a pony and trap. On the way home one of the two brothers decided to exercise his talents on the instrument, causing the horse to bolt and giving the two lads a frightening time. However, they did finally manage to bring the horse under control and proceeded home in a more subdued manner with the organ, luckily, still intact.

During the war years there were often as many as three fully-packed buses used

Basil Howse with one of his early buses.

on the Saturday 1.30 p.m. service. Passengers would stand all down the gangway and Mrs Paish, one of the conductresses, would shout from the front, 'All face this way please', thus enabling the maximum number of bodies to be 'packed in'. During this time Basil was using a bus that had a luggage rack on the roof. One evening on the late run home from Cheltenham, he was somewhat surprised to be stopped by the police. Unbeknown to him several of the lads from RAF Windrush had climbed up on top and, with their legs dangling over the sides, were enjoying a free ride home.

The young village lads enjoyed playing a joke on Basil. One evening, while on the late night run, he was driving a bus with an emergency exit at the rear. The seats on the bus were full and, as it was 'standing room only', one wag opened the emergency door and passengers filed out, made their way to the front entrance and reboarded. Basil, incredulous at the number of people that his bus could suddenly accommodate, didn't start to get suspicious until he saw the same faces for the third time! Realizing what was happening he chuckled, 'You young devils', and taking it all in good spirits, soon put things to rights. He was a very cheerful man with a great sense of humour and personality. He would oblige his passengers by picking them up and putting them down at their front gates.

Basil's buses were used extensively for outings, on all the village football team's away matches and also on school runs. When the empty quarters at Windrush camp were used as temporary accommodation for some Sherborne folk, their children still attended Sherborne School. Basil would pick them up each morning and drop them at the bottom end of the village on his way through to Clapton, where he picked up another busload of children for Sherborne School. At Christmas time Basil bought a poke bag full of sweets for each of the school children.

During the heavy snowfalls of 1947 the bus, on its return journey from Cheltenham, reached as far as the Puesdown Inn, and could go no further. The Northleach passengers decided to make their own way home as best they could, leaving bus driver Ted Fowler, conductress Mabel Harding and the only remaining passenger, eighty-year-old Mrs Edgington from Aldsworth. All three had to stay the night at the inn. The following day Ted and Mabel made their way on foot to Northleach, where they were met by Basil and transported back to Aldsworth. The bus and Mrs Edgington were forced to remain at the Puesdown Inn for a week, where the old lady helped with the washing up. Mrs Edgington's verdict on the whole affair 'It was the best holiday I've ever had!'

Over the years the bus drivers, apart from Basil and Ted Fowler were Ted Ball, Bill Haines, Ewart Cook, Ted Leather, Pip Curtis, Harry Smith and Jack Meadwell. Occasionally, Basil's son Cyril would help out in an emergency, but he also had his own very successful transport business to run. The conductors were George Johnson and Ernie Puffett, and the conductresses, apart from Mabel Harding who we have already mentioned, were Evelyn Paish, Dolly Howell, Kathy Broughton and Basil's daughter Joyce Cook. In 1952 Basil retired and sold the company to Marchants of Cheltenham, but the atmopshere was never the same; Basil's cheerful countenance was sadly missed.

Unfortunately we are left today with an almost non-existent bus service, partly due to the fall in demand and the large number of villagers with private cars.

Tommy and Mrs Lester lived behind Brook House in one of a row of cottages known now as Elm Tree Cottages. They kept a shop which sold cigarettes, sweets and a few groceries. Tommy, who had a petrol pump installed in his yard, used his lorry for a carrier service. The vehicle, equipped with a tarpaulin cover, was easily converted into a passenger carrier with the addition of a wooden seat down each side. It was often used to carry the village football team to away games before Basil Howse's bus was available. The lorry required pushing up steep hills, especially Fish Hill on the Evesham road, and it also needed the occasional tyre change because punctures were common. All these inconveniences were accepted in good spirits by the male passengers who would provide a helping hand.

Leslie Lester, Tommy's brother, ran a village taxi service for many years, and was also employed by the Hon. Mrs Charles Dutton (Lord Sherborne's mother).

Jinny Larner, another shopkeeper, also sold sweets, cigarettes and a few grocery items. She had another sideline, selling home-cooked fish and chips, which she prepared and cooked herself in one of the almshouse cottages. Jinny later moved to No. 47 where she carried on her trading.

Jack Dixon, who lived at the Bottom End of the village, was a part-time chimney sweep for the cottagers. His other abiding talent was his natural gift for 'charming away' warts.

Mrs Lucy Faulkner, a great friend of Lord and Lady Sherborne's, was the daughter of Lord Bray. With her brother, the Hon. Verney Cave, she lived in a flat at Lodge

Lucy Faulkner thatching the fishing lodge at Dodds Mill.

Park. During the war, Lucy, like the Sherbornes, was a member of the ATA. Mrs Faulkner was skilled as a thatcher and the only lady thatcher in Gloucestershire. She put this talent to good use when re-thatching the Dutton's fishing hut at Dodds Mill. Sadly both mill and hut have fallen prey to the ravages of time, and are both now demolished.

Mr and Mrs Taylor (old Fred and Else) kept the village shop and post office for many years. When Fred's parents married, their first home was at Waterloo (which was two houses at that time). His father worked as the electrician at Sherborne House, where he was eventually succeeded by Mr Hubbard. When Mr Hubbard left the village Fred took his place as electrician, having previously been employed on the estate in the forestry department. In 1922, when the first telephone was installed, Else assumed the management of the Sherborne and Windrush telephone switchboard. Five years later Fred and Else took over the village shop and in 1929, upon the death of Albert Townsend, they acquired the post office. Fred took a great interest in the sports and social life of the village, as Committee member for both the Cricket and Football Clubs, Chairman of the Parish Council and School Governor. He also loved to play a hand of whist.

The shop hours were as follows: open from 7.30 a.m. to 10 p.m. weekdays, as they held an off licence to sell bottled beer (Garnes) and cider (Woodpeckers), and closed from 1 p.m. until 6 p.m. on Saturdays, as it was the post office half-day closing.

During these days a large part of the diet of the working classes was hocks, bacon joints and cheese. Large, round cheeses were delivered whole to the shop, where they were cut up with wire cheese-cutters (a practice that continued here until 1990). Bacon was delivered a side at a time, complete with the hocks.

During the Second World War when military personnel occupied Sherborne House, the telephone switchboard required manning 'round the clock', so Fred and Else took turns to sleep beside it on a camp bed. When their son Harry left school, he assisted in running the business and delivering the weekly groceries to various homes until he was eventually 'called up' and served in the RAF Air Sea Rescue Service. Upon demobilization, he returned to the village to take up where he had left off, delivering the mail and the daily newspapers.

During the period when Sherborne House was occupied as King's School, some of the boys, on certain days of the week and only at specified times of the day, were allowed down to the shop to spend their pocket money. However, the odd 'escapee' could turn up at any hour!

When the new automatic telephone exchange (built near the school) was in service (c. 1957), the switchboard was removed from the shop. The Sherborne and Windrush telephone subscribers donated towards a gift of a silver salver in recognition of the Taylors' dedicated and loyal service. The salver was presented by Mr W.H. Limbrick at a reception at the home of Mr and Mrs Wilfred Mayes. In

Presentation of a silver salver to Mr and Mrs F. Taylor, centre, by Mr W.H. Limbrick, left, and Mrs A. Limbrick, right.

1956, Harry assisted by his wife Mavis, assumed control of the business under the watchful eyes of his parents. He eventually ceased the delivery of the newspapers. Bread and cakes, previously delivered house to house by the bakers from Northleach and Barrington, were delivered to the shop three times a week by a bakery firm from the Forest of Dean by 1974. This followed the closure of the local firms.

Both Mavis and Harry were very much involved in village life, Harry was a member of both the cricket and football teams, and he was Chairman of the Parish Council, a School Governor, a Church Warden and Secretary to the Parochial Church Council. Mavis was a member of the WI and the PCC. Harry eventually retired from delivering the Royal Mail and in November 1986, much to the dismay and sorrow of the villagers, sold the business complete with the living accommodation. In the previous month of October, during the harvest supper held in the Social Club in aid of church funds, the Hon. Juliet Dutton surprised both Taylors by presenting them with a clock and a pair of china bird ornaments. Mavis was also presented with a bouquet of flowers by Celia Limbrick. All the gifts resulted from donations by their customers and friends.

Harry and Mavis remained in residence in the village until July 1988, when they moved to Bourton-on-the-Water. However, they did not sever all ties with Sherborne; Harry is still a School Governor, Mavis is a member of the WI, and they both continue their allegiance to the church.

The Tremaine family have been farming Sherborne Farm for over a hundred years. Mr William H. Tremaine originally brought his family of nine children and their

Mr W.H. Tremaine and his family in 1897. Standing, left to right: Maud Mary, James, Lillian Jane, William, Jack Oliver. Front row, seated: Mabyn Gwendoline, William Hutchings, Gladys, Fanny Jane, Thomas Hedley, Rose Fanny.

Four young village lads in 1934. Left to right: Richard Tremaine, John Newport, William and James Tremaine.

nursemaid Jemima from Cornwall in 1887. Jemima later married Charles Taylor, a woodsman on the estate and they took up residence at No. 23 Sherborne. Mr Tremaine was a short, thick-set man with rosy cheeks, giving rise to his nickname of 'Chubby'. His usual method of transport was on horseback; he was frequently seen trotting through the village, sporting a black top hat. William was the first Chairman of the Parish Council, newly formed in 1894. He worked the farm with his son, also named William.

When William junior married, he continued to live in the farmhouse with his wife. They regularly attended church with their family, William was a church warden and often read the lesson on Sunday mornings. Sherborne farmhouse and gardens were regularly used for fund-raising events for the church.

Mr Tremaine was Chairman of the Parish Council for many years, a Committee Member of the Horticultural Society, the Cricket Club and the Sherborne Club.

William and James, grandsons of W.H. Tremaine, farm Sherborne and Sandyhill Farms to this day. Like their father and grandfather before them, they are regular attenders at church and are both members of the PCC. William is Church Warden, a member of the Parish Council and a School Governor, and James is Treasurer of the PCC. Together they run a milking herd of Friesians and rear calves for beef production on Sherborne Farm. They also have a flock of 260 lambs and 180 Border Leicester ewes which they cross with Suffolk rams, and thus keep up the old tradition of sheep farming in the village.

Jim Smith, born in 1908, is one of the oldest surviving inhabitants of the village. The eldest of a family of five children, four boys and one girl, Jim lived at Home Farm where his father was an employee. In 1920 both his parents died during an influenza epidemic. Despite being a widow, his maternal grandmother took charge of all five children and provided them with a home at the Top End of the village. To accommodate the family, cottages Nos 2 and 3 were incorporated into one dwelling.

At the age of thirteen, Jim was allowed to leave school to start work, with the poultry, on Home Farm. His work day was from 7 a.m. until 5 p.m. on weekdays and 7 a.m. to 1 p.m. on Saturdays, for which he was paid the sum of 10s. His tasks also included feeding and securing the poultry on Saturday afternoons, Sunday mornings and Sunday afternoons. When asked if he ever joined the other village boys for a game of football his reply was, 'No fear, there's no time for games, I've allus got a lot of b—dy work to do!' As he grew older he began to undertake more general farmwork, first with the horses and later with the tractor. Jim remembers very well the day the first tractor arrived on the farm, and the excitement that accompanied the occasion. Jim is one of the few old Gloucestershire characters remaining today in any of the villages. Some of his favourite replies to questions were 'Not as I knows on', 'Oh ah' and 'Summutt like that'.

When his grandmother died Jim moved to the Bottom End of the village to live with his aunt, Mrs Dixon. The other children lodged with families in the village or with relatives elsewhere. Jim's final move was to No. 83 where he still resides. Along with his workmates, Rolly and Cecil Harding, Jim walked to and from his workplace at Home Farm, every day for his entire working life. When prophesying the weather, he always maintains that if the wind is coming from the east on 21 March, it will remain in that quarter until 21 June. This has indeed proved true on many, many occasions.

Mark Cook, like Jim, is a true countryman. Although not born in Sherborne, he has lived in the village for many years in one of the cottages at The Oranges. Mark's wife, Rose Lockey, spent her childhood in one of the Woeful Lake cottages and attended the Sherborne village school. Until his retirement, Mark worked on the land as an employee of Geoff Houlton for many years, farming Mill Hill as well as Empshill Farm at Farmington. The fascinating craft of making corn dollies is Mark's favourite hobby, and despite being self-taught his finished products are exquisitely constructed. Now, as a resident of Northleach, he very much enjoys being a member of the Evergreen Club and is not averse to offering his talents when he can be of assistance.

Mark provided the following seasonal rhyme;

> January brings the snow,
> Makes one's feet and fingers glow.
> February fills the ditch,
> With black or white, I don't care which.
> March brings breezes loud and shrill
> And stirs the dancing daffodils.
> April brings the primrose sweet,

Scatters daisies at our feet.
May brings flocks of pretty lambs,
Skipping by their fleecy dams.
June brings tulips, lilies, roses,
To fill the children's hand with posies.
Hot July brings thunder showers,
Apricots and jilly flowers.
August brings us sheaves of corn,
Then the Harvest Home is born.
Warm September brings the fruit,
Sportsmen then begin to shoot.
Fresh October brings the pheasant,
When to gather nuts is pleasant.
Dull November brings the blast,
When the leaves are falling fast.
Chill December brings the sleets,
Blazing fires and Christmas treats.

Winnie George spent her childhood at Home Farm where her father, Arch Jones, was a carter when Mr Blake was bailiff to Lord Sherborne. As there were no other children at the farm, which is situated about half a mile from the village, Winnie spent her spare time in the company of the farm employees, and as she grew older, in her father's company with the horses. When Mr Broad retired as a shepherd in the 1920s, he was employed to keep the road from Home Farm to Cheltenham Lodges clear of leaves. As the road was lined with old beech trees, there was always plenty of sweeping to do, and lots to burn. Winnie remembers 'helping' Mr Broad with this task; she particularly loved stoking the fires along the route. Around 10 a.m. they would break for lunch, when Winnie and Mr Broad would share his slices of burnt toast spread with jam. If they were near the farm they would shelter in the shepherds hut, joining Jim Clark the farm shepherd. During lambing, the farmyard was made into a lambing pen with light supplied by a hurricane lamp. Winnie was given the job of feeding the sheep from a little galvanized bucket filled with rolled oats. She admits that she was probably more of a hindrance than a help to the shepherds, but they tolerated her presence quite happily. When she was older, Winnie would help her father with the horses, grooming and watering them, and cleaning the harness and brasses.

During haymaking and harvest time Win's days were spent leading the horses backwards and forwards between the fields and the hay or corn ricks. In the evening, when the day's work was done, she would ride the horses out to the fields to graze. Winnie has never lost her passion for horses, and even now she welcomes a rare day out at the races and avidly watches the race meetings on the television.

The following recipe, provided by Win, was copied by her mother in the early 1900s:

A Lovers' Cake

Take one small waist
One long arm
And a little hesitation
Stir slowly then add a little gentle squeeze
One head on shoulder
One 'May I?'
Two kisses, then allow it to simmer gently in the
Moonlight for about ten minutes
Then proceed to add a much tighter squeeze
Six kisses
Flavour with 'Dears' and 'Darlings'
Mix the whole in the shade.

Eileen Hill, an only child, was born in Sherborne. After leaving school she worked in Miller's Drapers in Northleach. Each day, regardless of the weather, Eileen would bicycle to and from her workplace in Northleach.

At the outbreak of the Second World War she had to register for war work. In 1941 she worked in the Maintenance Unit at RAF Little Rissington. Each day, Sundays included, Fluck's bus would collect the workers from the surrounding villages and transport them to their place of work. When the aircraft flew into Little Rissington for repair, Eileen's job was to log them in and out, and also to keep the hangar clean. Among the crippled craft brought in for repair were Spitfires, Halifaxes and Wellingtons.

She remembers Lord Sherborne and Amy Johnson bringing aircraft in for repair. Miss Johnson experienced great difficulty in locating the airfield, because it was so well camouflaged. Eileen married Billy, eldest son of Alan Hill, the estate gamekeeper. They eventually moved to Norfolk, where she still lives.

Just before the war, when domestic workers were much reduced in numbers, **Leslie Hayward** earned his pocket money by helping the butler at Sherborne House. The house staff then comprised the butler, the cook/housekeeper, three housemaids and one kitchen maid. By this time the large, old-fashioned kitchen was no longer in use, and the meals were prepared in the still room which had previously been used for making fancy cakes and pastries. Leslie's tasks included those jobs originally completed by the hall-boy and the footman. He carried water, in white enamel cans, to the male guests and members of the family. This they used for washing before going in to the dining room for meals. He also cleaned the cutlery and silver down in the ship hall, where a window overlooked the cemetery. Leslie found this quite a frightening place to be at night, especially when his thoughts turned to tales of the ghosts which were supposed to walk the passages. Any unusual sounds would result in the silver cleaning being abruptly curtailed and Leslie hurrying to find solace in the company of others! His other tasks included filling the copper log baskets that stood outside the library and sitting-room doors, closing the shutters around the house and checking that the front door was locked.

Wheelwright's yard at number one, Sherborne in the late 1930s. Left to right; Stewart Saunders, Maggie Saunders and Fred Saunders (wheelwright).

He also assisted with the washing up in the butler's pantry. As a choir boy he went to Sherborne House, where Lady Ethel Sherborne presented each member of the choir with a pair of gloves for Christmas and a chocolate egg at Easter. During the war Leslie served in the Royal Navy and on demobilization joined the building trade and now, with his eldest son David, runs his own building company. Leslie was a playing member of the Football Club and is still a member of the Parish Council.

Alf Margetts left the village school at the age of fourteen to start work in Sherborne House as a hall boy. He was the only village boy taken to 'live in'. He assisted the butler, cleaned the shoes and silver, and assisted the cook/housekeeper. He ran errands to the estate office which was situated at the Top End of the village. He also delivered jars of soup, supplied from the house kitchens, to the very elderly, retired and sick estate workers. Hip baths, used in the bedrooms by the Dutton family and guests, had to be filled and emptied. He remembers Mr Mosson, the coachman, collecting the daily newspapers from Bourton-on-the-Water and delivering the lunches, packed in hay boxes, to the shooting parties. During the 'Summer Season', while the Dutton family were in London, the drawing room carpet would be taken up and mounted on a scaffold erected on the bank outside the church, and the estate workers were employed to beat the dust out using canes similar to flat besoms. Alf also recalls the two Misses Timms, who were employed to scrub the stone passages and back portion of the house. They always went home laden with left-over food provided by the kitchens. In time Alf was promoted to footman. This position required that he spend the 'Summer Season' in London with the Dutton family, where he often caught a glimpse of the Queen and Princess Margaret when they were children.

CHAPTER ELEVEN

Snippets

We have collected together under this heading a variety of interesting bits and pieces relating to the village over the years. They are taken from wills, tombstones, advertisements, petitions, diaries and other village records and listed chronologically.

1566 – 'The Act for Nets and Shrapes' (the destruction of choughs, crows and rooks) was revived and the following rates were fixed:
Heads of old birds: three for one penny.
'Chawks', crows, pyes or rooks: six young for one penny.
For unbroken eggs: six for one penny, they must not be taken or destroyed with hand-guns or crossbow.
The price of a fox: twelve pence.
For each head of a bullfinch or other bird that devours the 'blowth' of fruit: one penny (Statutes of the Realm).

1614 – Extract from the copy of the will of Elizabeth Dutton (Elizabeth was not a 'Sherborne House Dutton'). To her son, Richard, she left:
 £13 13s. 4d.
 2 pieces of pewter
 1 white candlestick
 1 pair of flaxen sheets
 1 flock bed
 2 bolsters
 the best black coverlid
 1 brass pan
 2 napkins
To her daughter, Ann, she left:
 her best petticoat
 1 double kerchief
 2 pieces of pewter
 1 billow bier of the 2nd sort
 1 pair of sheets
 2 table napkins
 1 old thin sheet
 1 old apron
To her son, William Junior, she left:
 1 old thin tablecloth.

1616 – Charities: Alexander Reid, Vicar of Sherborne from 1569 to 1616, donated £40 in Trust to provide for the marriages of two poor girls and to help the aged householders.

In the late seventeenth century the charity yielded £13 per year, and another £15 was donated by various people 'for the poor'. All of these charities were lost by 1828.

1630 – A Petition of the parishioners of Wyck Rissington, to the House of Commons, complaining of their vicar the Revd Robert Knollys. The living was worth £100 yearly.

For the past five years he has neither read prayers nor prayed in the Parish Church. He employs the cheapest Curates he can get irrespective of principles or evil and loose life. The Sacrament has not been administered upon the days appointed and very seldom or never has there been any Sermon on Sunday or prayers on week-days; and since Christmas for four Sundays at a time, there has been no Church Service whatever. A woman of the Parish could not obtain spiritual consolation on her death-bed, and when she died her husband had to entreat the Parson of another Parish to come and bury her.

1638 – Lucy Dutton, aged fourteen years, youngest daughter of John Dutton (the hunchback) married the Earl of Downe, aged sixteen years. Both died while still comparatively young; she in 1656, aged only thirty-one, and the Earl in 1660, aged thirty-eight years.

1642 – An order was made, by the House of Lords, for the apprehension of Sir Ralph Dutton of Standish for beating up a drum for soldiers in Gloucestershire and Herefordshire. The Under Sheriff of Gloucester, with ten Parliamentarians, set upon Sir Ralph Dutton and ten Cavaliers, but Sir Ralph escaped by swimming across the River Severn.

1674 – The Curate of Aldsworth 'married' at all hours of the day and night without banns, licence or other formality. He realized approximately £80 per year by the business.

1723 – Plants and fruit trees supplied to Sherborne Gardens totalled £13 11s. 9d. These consisted of 'Dutch and Brussels Apricots, Hypatnine and Blue Peaches, figs etc. Plants, Sweet Briars, Scorpion Senas, Atlheas (Hollyhocks), Spanish Broom, Alliacks, Polyanthus, Bellflowers and Tuberose'.

1772 – September. Extract from the will of James Lenox Dutton, 'He was to be buried in the family Vault at Sherborne at midnight, and his body to be borne and attended by his own servants and no others'.

1844 – A tombstone near the church was erected in memory of the Sherborne House housekeeper, Frances Trinder, who died 14 January 1844, aged seventy-five years. Its inscription reads: 'Forty years housekeeper to Lord and Lady Sherborne by whom this stone is erected to commemorate her upright Christian character, and to mark their gratitude for her faithful and affectionate services to the end of her life, and to their attachment to a valued servant and friend'.

1866 –   One sheep 96 lbs cost £3 4s. 0d.
         One Hindquarter of Beef 167 lbs cost £4 17s. 5d.
         One Spring Lamb cost 6s.
         One Pig 297 lbs cost £7 1s. 2d.

1866 –   13 April. Charlie Jones walked to Sherborne from Windrush 'elping among the sheep' and then planted barley in the field and two rows of potatoes (American Roses).

1886 –   27 December to 9 January 1887. 'Very heavy snowfalls and frost'.

1894 –   4 December. The first parish meeting was called. Mr W.H. Tremaine was elected Chairman and the following seven were elected as Parish Councillors by a showing of hands.
         Mr Frederick Beeman (Vice-Chairman)
         Mr George Freeman (District Councillor)
         Mr William Hooper
         Revd Edward Kirby
         Mr William Pitts
         Mr Robert Slade
         Mr George Stevens

1896 –   An earthquake tremor was felt.

1900 –   Funeral expenses: Coffin £2 5s. 0d.
                            Grave Digger 4s.
                            Bearers 8s.

1925 –   Clem Jones purchased a cart horse for £25.

1935 –   6 May. Silver Jubilee Celebrations (an extract from Parish Council minutes)

On a beautifully fine day and by kind permission of Lord and Lady Sherborne, festivities were held in the grounds of Sherborne Park, to commemorate the occasion of the Silver Jubilee of HM King George V and HM Queen Mary. The festivities commenced with the ringing of the church bells followed by the radio broadcast of the National Thanksgiving Service from St Paul's Cathedral. In the afternoon parishioners assembled on the lawns of Sherborne House, and after singing the National Anthem, Lady Sherborne presented each child with a Jubilee Mug. Tea was provided for all and an excellent programme of sports and games for both adults and children took place. Balloons were released at intervals. Those parishioners who were unable to attend, through illness, were not forgotten and tea was sent to them. During the evening, beer and bread and cheese were provided and a display of fireworks brought a very pleasant day to a conclusion.

1940 – 1,000 cartridges cost £7 10s. 0d.
      1 chauffeur's new navy blue suit cost £6 10s. 0d.
      1 pair of gloves, purchased from B.P. Hannis of Bourton-on-the-Water, cost 11s. 6d.

1945 – May. (From a newspaper cutting)

Pte E. Margetts arrived back to a warm welcome after being a prisoner of war for 3 years. Teddy, as he is familiarly known, was captured at Knightsbridge, Tobruk, and sent to Italy. After Italy capitulated he was free for a month before being caught by the Italian Police and handed over to the Germans. He was taken to Stalag VIIIB camp and then to a working camp in Poland where he worked for a year in coal mines. On January 19th, 1945 due to the advance of the Russians, a group of thirty prisoners, with five or six guards, started on their 1,000 mile march across Europe into Germany. While crossing the bridge into Regensburg they were bombed by the Americans. Some of the prisoners were killed, Teddy was injured in the head by shrapnel. Nights were spent in whatever shelter they could find and they fed on potatoes, swedes and turnips or what could be obtained from farmers. They were released by the Americans just outside Regensburg in May, taken into Belgium and finally transported in British bombers home to England.

1946 – Mr Fred Taylor was granted a wayleave to use the Nissen hut in the front field for the sole purpose of a garage for the rent of £1 per annum (the Nissen hut had been erected during the war for the purpose of storing emergency rations). It has now been demolished.

1947 – 5/6 March. Very heavy snowfalls, the worst blizzard in living memory. The village was completely isolated for three or four days. Mr W. Limbrick consented to Cecil Vincent and David Margetts using two of his tractors and a small wagon to make their way across the fields to Windrush to meet Joe Leach and his son Peter (bakers from Great Barrington). They brought back as much bread as was physically possible. This was taken to the village shop, run by Mr and Mrs Taylor, and from there it was distributed to the villagers.

1948 – November. Mains electricity supply was connected to Stones Farm and No. 55 Sherborne.
      Erection of two telephone kiosks in the village, one at each end.

1949 – Mains electricity was connected to the remainder of the village.

1950 – Two notice boards were erected, one at each end of the village.

1952 – The mobile library started its fortnightly journeys around the north Cotswold villages.

1953 – 28 March. The foxhounds met in the village and, while they were moving off, Mrs Margett's hat blew off among them. The huntsmen halted in their tracks, while one gallant rider dismounted, retrieved the offending article and returned it to its rather embarrassed owner.

June. The Coronation celebrations of Queen Elizabeth II opened with a service in the church and the exciting news that Edmund Hilary and Sherpa Tensing had conquered Mount Everest. The villagers gathered in the homes of those fortunate enough to have a television set, to watch the service in Westminster Abbey. Due to the very wet conditions, the planned outdoor activities had to be cancelled. Teas were provided in the school and photographs were taken of all those present. In the evening the parishioners gathered on the disused airfield at Windrush to witness a display of fireworks and bonfires.

1954 –   6 February. Identical twins, Joan and Jean Adams, married identical twins, Cyril and Sidney Tidmarsh of Great Barrington, in Sherborne church.

The twelve Council houses built along the Haycroft Road were occupied by those who had been living in temporary accommodation at Windrush Camp.

1960s –   During this period a mains water supply and mains sewerage were connected into the village.

1967 –   February. The Russian Sputnik was sighted by villagers.

Towards the end of the 1960s, the weekly surgery, held in the village on Wednesday mornings by the Bourton-on-the-Water doctors, came to an end due to new NHS regulations and the amalgamation of the Northleach and Bourton-on-the-Water medical practices. Over the years, the venue for the surgery had been Nos 39, 47 and, lastly 46 Sherborne.

1969 –   20 July. While millions of people around the world watched the historic lunar landing by American astronauts, at least two ladies in Sherborne refused to believe that the operation had taken place, preferring instead to believe it was a hoax set up in the television studios!

1970 –   Shell Mex Oil Co. drilled for oil near the A40 at Radbourne's Corner field on Home Farm. When no oil was found the hole was filled and made safe.

1973 –   (approximately). Mr Jack Saunders, a seventy-four-year-old retired gardener, was the *Sunday People*'s 'Marrow Master of Great Britain'. Jack's monster marrow weighed in at 34 lbs. He won £50 in cash, and a silver cup which was held for a year. He was quoted as saying that he had been growing marrows since he left school. Messrs Suttons Seeds were the co-sponsors of the competition. Our research has failed to pin down the exact date but Jack and his wife Eva were to have a second taste of stardom later when they were featured in a television gardening programme and their garden was chosen as a typical 'old cottage garden', containing hives of bees among the flowers, fruit and vegetables.

1977 –   June. Several trees, including maple, were planted by Lady Joan Sherborne in the top corner of the school playing field to commemorate the Silver Jubilee of Queen Elizabeth II. Also, the Jubilee Wood (consisting of

MARROW MASTER

By ANTHONY HUXLEY

JACK SAUNDERS, a 74-year-old retired gardener who has been growing marrows since he left school, is the Sunday People's Marrow Master of Great Britain.

That's Jack pictured left with his monster marrow, which weighs 34 lb. He wins the first prize of a silver cup to be held for a year, and £50 in cash.

Jack lives at Sherborne, near Cheltenham. Mr. Bryan Debenham, of Bury St. Edmunds, was second and wins £25.

The five runners-up, Mr. E. V. Howes, of Trowbridge, Wiltshire; Mr. W. Woodhouse, of Penrith, Cumberland; Mrs. I. M. Plummer, of Hordle, Lymington, Hants; Mr. G. E. Gibbons, of Wellingborough, Northants; and Mr. D. Pearce, of Coseley, near Bilston, Staffs, will each receive a £5 voucher from Suttons Seeds, co-sponsors of the contest.

Jack Saunders with his monster marrow.

nine different species of trees) was planted in front of Sherborne House by the estate woodsmen.

1988 – March. A television documentary on the lives of identical twins, featuring Mr and Mrs C. Tidmarsh and Mr and Mrs S. Tidmarsh and families, was filmed and later shown on television.

8 November. An oak tree was planted at the end of the school playground to replace the magnolia planted in 1968, which did not survive; a beech tree was also planted in the corner of the playing field on the same day. Both trees were planted by Mr Harry Taylor, ex-Chairman of the Parish Council, to commemorate the centenary of the forming of the Gloucestershire County Council. Also present were the school staff, pupils and governors, Lady Dunrossil (a Gloucestershire County Councillor) and members of the Parish Council.

November. At the monthly meeting of the Parish Council, Mr Walter Tufnell, the newly elected Chairman, presented Harry Taylor with a cut glass decanter in appreciation of the twenty years he had spent as Chairman of the Parish Council and the long years of service he had given to the village.

1989 – The National Trust assumed full control of the Sherborne estate, appointing Mr Andrew Mayled as resident warden.

With the passing of the years, the number of estate workers had dwindled from eighty-nine in 1911 to just eight in 1989; Ken James, Michael

Robinson, Edward Jewell and Victor (Snowy) Strange in the forestry department; Robin Yaxley as painter; Roy Shaw and Patrick Henley responsible for maintenance; and Albert Henley as groundsman at Lodge Park.

Royal Visits to Sherborne

1282 – King Edward I visited the manor.

1574 – Queen Elizabeth I spent a few days at Sherborne House. She was visiting from her hunting lodge at Langley in Wychwood Forest.

1592 – Queen Elizabeth I visited again and was greeted by William Dutton. Charles II (who reigned from 1660 to 1685) and Nell Gwyn are said to have visited the coursing pavilion at Lodge Park.

1681 – Charles II's illegitimate son, the Duke of Monmouth, visited Sherborne.

1788 – George III visited Sherborne House on his way to Cheltenham.
         In the early nineteenth century the Prince Regent, while attending the races at Bibury, stayed at Sherborne.

Crimes

Like most villages, Sherborne has not escaped its share of crime. Here are a few examples over the centuries:

1340 – Several tenants were fined for taking cloth to be 'fulled' outside the manor lands.

1785 – Henry Stevens of Clapton, yeoman, was convicted of using dogs to kill game at Sherborne and was fined £20.

1793 – Thomas Cockhead of Black Bourton, yeoman, was convicted of using dogs and net to kill game at Sherborne and was fined £5.

1800 – Martin Turner, mason, and John Winfield and Joseph Cook, labourers, all of Burford, were fined £20 for using nets to kill hares at Sherborne.

1806 – William Still of Aston Blank was fined £5 for using snares to kill game at Sherborne.

Epilogue

When we first set out, as complete amateurs, to record the history of our village, we had no idea of the size of the task that we had undertaken. We have, however, been pleased and encouraged by the response and by the help received in gathering so much information on life in the past.

With so many of the 'good things in life' lost with the passage of time, nostalgia has inevitably crept into much of what has been written. We apologize for portraying some families more than others, but this resulted because of the information we had to hand, coupled with the small number of senior, original inhabitants of the village we had to talk to and, sadly also to lapses of memory.

Alas, like other villages, we have now lost the service of most door-to-door tradesmen, the only exceptions being the milkman and 'Mr Fish' (purveyor of wet fish), who still calls on request.

Our newspapers, instead of being delivered to the door, are now left at three collection points: No. 28 Sherborne, the home of Mr and Mrs A. Bunting; No. 53 Sherborne, the home of Mr and Mrs K. James; and the village post office.

Thanks to Paul and Penny Collins we are extremely lucky to retain the facility of a village shop and Post Office. This supplies us with all the daily essentials and many little luxuries too, and always served with a smile and good cheer.

We still have an active village school with one of the teachers residing in Sherborne, and an active church although, regrettably, not as active as it was in yesteryear.

Despite all the changes, for better and for worse, the village still retains its rural character, with virtually unspoiled panoramic views of great beauty (especially enjoyed by visitors). The delightful brook still meanders sleepily through the fields and pastures where sheep and lambs graze peacefully upon its banks, much as it was in the days of yore.

We hope enough has been recounted to give some idea of life as it was lived and to tell of the changes which have taken place, especially in the last century, in this lovely old village in the Cotswolds.

Glossary
Gloucestershire Terms and Sayings

'If through Gloucestershire you be, "I" pronounce the double "e".' As such, feet becomes fit, sheep becomes ship and seeds become sids.

Allus –	Always
Arter –	After
B'aint –	Is not
Byent –	Are not
Bissent –	Are not
Bwoy –	Boy
Chimbley –	Chimney
Chimmock –	Chimney
Cyart –	Cart
Darricky –	Rotten
Dang –	Darn or damn
Ent –	Have not
Er –	She
Fer flummoxed –	Didn't understand
Forrard –	Forward
Fust –	First
Fuddled –	Muddled
Farty –	Forty
Fower –	Four
Ketch –	Catch
Ower –	Our
Oss –	Horse
Okkard –	Awkward
Summat –	Something
Stwun –	Stone
Shupperd –	Shepherd
Secertery –	Secretary
Tith –	Teeth
Twunt –	It won't
Tud –	It would
Thur –	There
Uffor –	Before
Ud –	Would

Ull –	Will
Wur –	Where
Wuth –	Worth
Yead or Yud –	Head
Yer –	Here
Yen it –	Isn't it
It yent –	It isn't
Yups –	Heaps

Sayings

Quarten of tay –	A quarter of tea
Boughten cake –	A shop cake
Dought the lamp or fire –	Put out the lamp or fire
He's a gert big un you –	It's a big one
How b'ist thee –	How are you
Middlin –	Poorly
Fair to middlin –	Not too bad
Long headed bloke –	Intelligent man
Watty handed –	Left handed
Tother one –	The other one
I bet thee cassant –	I bet you can't

A True Conversation

An elderly villager met a young woman in a hurry.
  Villager: 'Bist thee goin to catch that ther bus?'
  Young woman: 'As a matter of fact I am.'
  Villager: 'Well thee bent then 'cos 'e's gone!'

Acknowledgements

This book would not have been possible without the help of a great number of people, including past and present inhabitants and a few complete strangers.

We are especially grateful to Mr J. Herrin, who allowed us full use of his private research of the village history, to Mr R. Rodgers for enduring our many intrusions into the school to peruse the old log books and to Mr J. Howarth of the National Trust.

Special thanks are due to Mrs Oakley, of Oxford, for the loan of the Dutton family photograph album and other material relevant to Sherborne House, to Mr W. Tremaine for allowing the use of his family album, and to Mr Richard Garne, who gave permission to quote any relevant information from his book *Cotswold Yeomen and Sheep*.

Our most grateful thanks go to the following for the loan of their precious photographs or for supplying useful information, support and enthusiasm: Mr A. Ash, Mr P. Ash, Mrs E. Belcher, Mr T. Boucher, Mr A. Bunting (Windrush), Mr P. Brown, Mr K. Chandler, Mr E. Cook, the late Mrs J. Cook, Mr M. Driver, Mr J. Fielding, Mr J. Fisher, Mrs W. George, Mr C. Gorton, Mrs B. Hall, Mr and Mrs B. Hall, Mr and Mrs W. Hayward, Mrs M. Herrin, Mrs E. Hill, Miss M. Holtham, Miss E. Houlton, Mr S. Irby, Mr K. James, Mrs Kelsey, Mr E. Jewell, Mrs M. Larner, Mr C. Lester, Mr W. Limbrick, Mr R. Limbrick, Mr A. Margetts, Mr and Mrs D. Margetts, Mr and Mrs E. Margetts, the late Mr F. Margetts, Mr M. Margetts, Mrs M. Mate, Mr K. Minns, Mr J. Newport, Mr T. Oakey, Mr and Mrs W. Petrie, Mrs D. Preston, Mr S. Renn, the late Mrs E. Robinson, Mr W. Rigsby, Mr B. Saunders, Mrs M. Saunders, Mrs E Seaman, Miss J. Shirley, Mrs D. Stevens, Mr J. Smith, Mr G. Simms, Mr and Mrs H. Taylor, Mr D. Thompson, Mr J. Tremaine, Miss B. Tufnell, Miss L. Tufnell, Mr P. Tufnell, Mr N. Turner, Mr D. Viner, Mrs J. Yaxley, the Cheltenham and Moreton-in-Marsh Libraries and the Cotswold Countryside Collection, Northleach.

Finally, we wish to thank Mr H. Sambo for reprinting and clarifying the many precious photographs and Mr P. Collins for retyping the original manuscript.

Bibliography

Domesday Book
Kelly's Directory 1856 to 1927
The *Victoria County History of Gloucestershire*
Samuel Rudder's History of Gloucestershire
Gloucester Records Office (various)
Gloucestershire Subsidy Roll 1327
Sherborne Muniments Book
Country Life; an article by Clive Aslet
The Cotswolds edited by Charles and Alice Mary Hadfield, David and Charles, Newton Abbot, Devon (1973)
The King's England, Gloucestershire by Arthur Mee, Hodder and Stoughton (1938)
Men and Armour for Gloucestershire in 1608